Mountain Biking For Women

Mountain Biking
For Women

Robin Stuart & Cathy Jensen

Acorn Publishing
Waverly, New York

Photographs by Cathy Jensen

Library of Congress Cataloging-in-Publication Data

Stuart, Robin.
    Mountain biking for women / Robin Stuart & Cathy Jensen.
        p.   cm.
    Includes bibliographical references (p.) and index.
    ISBN 0-937921-54-8
    1. Cycling for women. 2. All terrain cycling. I. Jensen, Cathy
II. Title
GV1057.S78 1994
796.6'082—dc20   94-27396
                                                                 CIP

Second printing—1995

Published by Acorn Publishing
Waverly, New York 14892

Printed in the United States of America

To Kim, who thought we'd enjoy mountain biking. Mahalo.

Contents

Acknowledgements

We would like to thank a bunch of folks for their guidance, moral support, and for appreciating our enthusiasm and not laughing at us. Scott (Taylor), Tom, Darcy, Steve and the rest of the guys at the Windsurf Bicycle Warehouse in South San Francisco, CA; our friend and model Julie Hall (and her patient fiancee, Michael); the Wednesday night gang: Julie, Jim, Sheila, Donald, the other Jim, Rick (and Mona) and anyone else who cares to join us; the good people at *Mountain Biking*, *Mountain Bike Action*, *Mountain Bike*, and *Bike* magazines for feeding our frenzy on a monthly basis; the millions of women who are turning to mountain biking in record numbers; and Dick Mansfield, for turning an exorcism of winter into a book.

We would like to give special thanks to some special people for their assistance and support: Jacquie Phelan and WOMBATS; Susan DeMattei of Diamond Back Racing; Delaine Fragnoli of *Mountain Biking Magazine*; Jan Bolland, Lisa Muhich, and David Townsend of Team Evian; Alison Sydor and Jennifer Prosser of the Volvo/Cannondale team; and Georgena Terry of Terry Precision Bicycles For Women.

"You're never completely out of the woods."

Jacquie Phelan
Three-time National Cross-country champion
Co-founding member of NORBA

Chapter 1

Introduction

Welcome to our world. It's a world of beauty, grace, and revelation. It is also a world of adrenaline, sweat, and redemption. There is a magic in the sport of mountain biking that we would like to share with you. The choices you have made that have brought us together may, quite literally, change your life - or not. Everything depends on you.

We will not only introduce you to mountain biking, we also will pass on some riding tips and handling maneuvers that you wouldn't know unless someone told you. Consider us 'someone'.

The techniques we will discuss were proven on Robin as coached by Cathy who was, as a pre-teen, one of the first amateur women off-road motorcycle racers. And, as her trophy collection indicates, she was one of the best. Under Cathy's tutelage, Robin, who could barely walk and chew gum at the same time, has become a mountain biking maniac.

We address this book to women, not out of some gleeful sexist bent, but because we are women and as such, understand things that a man might not.

We understand that the riding styles of the average man are different from the average woman. Women tend to be overly safety conscious where men can appear fearless.

We understand that most bikes you see at a bike shop are built with a 180 pound rider in mind, and therefore certain modifications or upgrades will have a markedly different effect on a lighter-weight rider. Crank arms, seat posts, handlebars and bar ends are engineered to withstand the abuse of someone twice our size. These same parts, forged from aluminum or titanium, are potentially more beneficial to us for they are notorious for bending and breaking under the weight of male riders. Such parts might last us a lifetime.

We understand that when learning the finer points of riding, one is not necessarily interested in starting with the history of the wheel. And we understand that not everyone gets a kick out of flying down trails at increasingly reckless speeds, just to see what will happen if they do not use their brakes.

After traversing many a trail, we have come to understand other, more subtle things that someone else might not take the time to notice or appreciate. For instance, rounding a turn on a wooded single-track and being struck by the primeval beauty of the sunlight sifting through the trees, shimmering off a rocky waterfall. Or, the captivating sense of awe when, upon finally reaching a mountain-top, you behold a panorama of rugged wilderness. By taking the time to observe as you ride, you'll discover the dramatic, beautiful elements in your surroundings that are easily overlooked by those possessed with the misguided drive to make every ride a race.

While the tranquility of a back country brook can take your breath away, on the trail you will also encounter more physical experiences. And they can be just as revelatory. You can get an undeniable rush from hammering a downhill at top speed. There's a moment of perfect clarity when the endorphins kick in while powering up a long or steep climb; your body moves seemingly devoid of effort while your mind and spirit transcend, enveloping you with every sight, sound, and motion occurring around you. The exhilaration of a sweeping cross-country downhill is better than any roller coaster, unhampered by obstacles or fear.

You see, mountain biking can be more than mere sport. It can be a lifestyle, filled with the lessons and valuable experiences that put you more in tune with yourself and the world of which we are all a part. It's about accomplishment, awareness, potential, and achievement. It's about freedom, politics, ethics, and mechanics. You get the idea.

The people involved in mountain biking are some of the nicest in the world. Let's face it, while you may come across a few jerks on mountain bikes, as a rule bad people do not pursue a state of grace. We've found a grace in mountain biking that elevates life above the mundane world of work, and bills, and CNN. That world is light years away whether you are cruising past a herd of Holsteins on a dirt road in Vermont or whizzing down the Slickrock Trail in Utah. Mountain biking offers something to everyone. The adrenaline junkie, the sun bunny, the racer, and the weekend warrior — all are created equal in the saddle.

Getting Started

If it has been a while since you have ridden a bike, don't worry; the old saying is true. You never forget how to ride. Now, it's only a matter of getting really good at it. The more you ride, the better you get, period. There are no shortcuts. Nobody just hops on a bike, ready to hammer their first time out. The human body is an amazing instrument, but it has to be tuned to play well.

The best thing you can do for yourself is to give your body time; time to get accustomed to riding, time to get in shape. You will be surprised at how little time it actually takes if you keep at it.

If you are fortunate enough to live near a park or a prime trail or two, become a regular visitor. Practice on smooth and level roads or trails at first; cruise around your neighborhood or do laps at your local playing field. Work on technique (See Chapters 3,4 & 5), and as you gain confidence, add some hills and trails. During the spring and summer months, make the most of the longer days. Try to fit in some after-work tootling at least a couple of nights a week. If you can, intersperse excursions of an hour or longer one night with shorter thirty to forty minute spins the nights before and after. All of this practice during the week gets you into shape for the weekends, when you can make a day of it.

Make time to ride on a regular basis, just for the practice, if for no other reason. Practice translates to experience while experience is directly related to confidence.

Confidence plays a large role in off-road riding. Some people mistakenly think it is all you need. Those people tend to crash a lot. You also need skill. Which is not to say you will not fall some time, too. But with skill, you will land well and maybe get a bruise. Without it, the landing may be a little harsher. We'll teach you all that later on.

Confidence is not only associated with your own capabilities but also with those of your trusted two-wheeled friend. We urge everyone to get on intimate terms with their bikes. By looking closely at it, learning how everything works, and performing the cleaning and periodic maintenance covered in Chapter 12, you will get to know your bike's personality, its quirks and strengths. The more you know, the deeper your trust that your bike will not let you down. Thus, the better you will ride.

Where To Get Information

Let's not mince any words. Your best resource for advice and information is your local bike shop. If you are serious enough about mountain biking to read this book, find a good bike shop and patronize it. The bike shop can be to riders what the lodge is to skiers. It is a meeting place where you have something in common with every other person there. It is a place to share your successes and failures, your dreams and near misses, to hear about new trails and learn new techniques, and to learn more about your bike.

At first glance, you can immediately distinguish the casual consumer from the true enthusiast. Their excitement is palpable and contagious; you can almost watch their pupils dilate when they walk through the door, especially if new bike models have recently arrived. Enthusiasts often are the shop employees themselves or they may be newcomers seeking advice and support. Ultimately, all of us are there for the same reason, for the love of the sport.

A bike shop is your best source of services, products, and information.

Aside from the camaraderie, bike shops are obviously your best source of services, products and information. They sell not only bikes, parts and accessories, but also videos, books, maps and magazines. Most shops are knowledgeable about local clubs, tour groups, land access organizations, and upcoming races. Regardless of what you need to know, they can point you in the right direction.

A decent bike shop is a mere flip through the yellow pages away. We realize that they are not like corner stores; depending on where you live, it may take a little doing to find one. But we have been from one coast to the other and our first quest in any town is to check out the local shop to see how they measure up. And you know what? The accents change, the focus may differ, but we have not been let down yet. In some cases, people are just dying to talk about their favorite pastime but there is nobody asking.

Once you have found a shop, and we are not talking about a department store that sells bikes along with a million other items — we mean an honest-to-goodness, that is all they sell and do, bike shop — take a little walk-through. The biggest retail day of the week for all stores including bike shops is Saturday. If you are curious and want to see what they have to offer but you do not necessarily want or expect to talk to anyone, Saturday is a good day to check a store out. Listen up as the staff works with customers. Are they taking their time and do they know what they are talking about? Or are they condescending to neophytes? If you like what you see and hear, go back for some advice and information on a weekday or an evening.

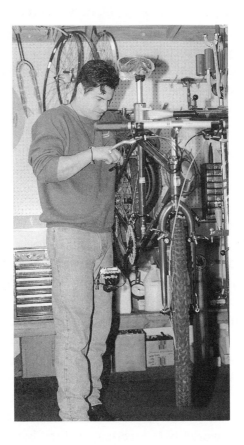

Ask bike mechanics, "What do you ride?"

If you are like we were and you want to learn all about "bike stuff," just walk in and start pointing and asking questions. Eavesdrop on conversations, especially between bike mechanics and someone who is shooting the breeze. As mountain bikers are a friendly lot, often times you can jump right into other people's conversations.

A great question, especially directed to mechanics, is "What do you ride?" You can get a crash course in the latest and hottest technology. As the terms start flying, do not be afraid to ask "What is that?" or "How do you like that?" Who can resist such an avid audience? You'll be there all afternoon.

We are aware of the unfortunate phenomenon of certain male enthusiasts and mechanics who talk down to or otherwise intimidate women. Don't put up with it — there are plenty of other sources of bicycle information and equipment. One tactic is to do your homework: digest a couple of issues of the bike magazines, cover-to-cover. Read this book from start to finish. You will then be prepared to hold your own with these guys. The best way to handle it, though, is to move on, accepting that there are good people and bad people, and do not assume the bad ones speak for everybody. To the sport's credit, we have only encountered less than five of these guys in all our travels.

If you are looking for parts or accessories and you know exactly what you want, check out the mail order scene as an option. However, never pump bike shop employees for all sorts of advice and then go out to a discount store or mail order firm for the gear. That is not only tactless, but hurts the professional shop that is giving full service to all customers.

You can also "ride the information highway" and pick up some good advice on what to ride and where to ride it. The Internet has several active newsgroups that discuss all aspects of cycling. It's a great place to ask, "I just saw this mountain bike called a Gazelle. Anyone know much about it?" You will likely get lots of advice from all over the country, if not the world. In the same vein, commercial networks like America On-Line have forums where you can ask the industry experts and other cyclists about what kind of saddle to buy, which tires work best in the mud, or what the best mountain bike buy is for under $600.

It still comes back to this: We recommend that you hook up with a local bike shop. As a rule of thumb, the most professional shops have employees who can impart their wisdom to all polite customers. The best bike shop people will seem like old friends. We have found that when a person, male or female, acts genuinely interested, the good bike folks (who make up the majority) brand that person "cool" and they will gladly tell you or show you anything you want to know. They'll go out of their way to get you up and riding on a mountain bike that fits both you and your budget.

"Every woman deserves a bike that fits and cycling shorts without a center seam."

Delaine Fragnoli
Associate Editor, *Mountain Biking Magazine*

Chapter 2

Mountain Bikes and Equipment

Types of Bikes

We figure that if you bought this book, it's a safe bet that you already have a bike. But, if you do not own a mountain bike, or if you have been bitten by the bug and you're thinking of upgrading to a new bike, here are some things you should know. First, there are two major questions you need to ask:

What do I plan to do with the mountain bike?

How much money am I willing to pay?

Let's take the second question first. We recommend that you buy the best bike that you can afford. A responsive light-weight bike properly tuned-up and sized for you will be a joy to ride — you'll love it. It also will hold up so that if you are out navigating over some rough terrain, miles from the trailhead, you'll have confidence that it will get you home.

You may not know, until you get started in earnest, where you may be riding. It may be around the block on pavement or on easy jogging trails; it may be on single-track many miles from the closest tarmac. Any bike can be ridden on pavement but only a special breed is made for the rigors of off-road adventures.

A responsive light-weight mountain bike is a joy to ride.

On a random Thursday morning, while walking through downtown San Francisco, Robin decided to count the bike messengers by bike type. She was curious about which style was favored among those who spend all day, five days a week, on two wheels. Not surprisingly, the ride of choice is a mountain bike. In a fifteen minute period, Robin counted twenty-five mountain bikes, four road bikes and one hybrid.

For those who may have blinked between 1990 and 1992, a hybrid is a bike that is a cross between a road bike and a mountain bike. Their intended use was primarily as a beefy road bike that could be taken on gentle off-road trails with a reasonable degree of confidence.

Mass production and marketing of true hybrids was fairly short-lived due to the undeniable fact that road riding and trail riding are decidedly different disciplines, requiring different equipment. A mountain bike's geometry is designed for agility, with an extra chainring for versatility; a large range of gear ratios allows for extreme variances in terrain. The frames are small and durable. Road bikes are designed to be primarily aerodynamic. The frames are larger, lightweight and built for speed.

In attempting to cross-breed the two disciplines (hence the name), manufacturers designed hybrids, which bore more resemblance to road bikes than mountain bikes. These bikes could perform both functions, but neither of them particularly well. However, the consumer response proved there was a niche market. Many manufacturers have created a "city" model of their mountain bikes, to satisfy both the industry critics and the buying public. This bicycle has a mountain bike frame with smaller, smoother tires and lower-end (i.e., heavier or less durable) components that can be easily upgraded for the bike to perform as a full-scale, off-road ready mountain bike.

If your intention is to get away from the citified pavement and explore the wilds of nature, we recommend real, meant-to-get-dirty mountain bikes. While upgrading a "city" bike is easy, as we said, it can get rather pricey. The cost of conversion may, when added to the city bike's cost, become more expensive than a mountain bike of similar quality. You are best off starting with what you want in the first place.

Bike Dealers vs. Discount or Department Store

With the cost of factory-made mountain bikes ranging from under $200 to over $3,000, it is natural to look for bargains. But don't expect to find huge savings on quality bikes — just like any piece of quality outdoor gear, be it a tent, a sleeping bag, or a backpack, you tend to get what you pay for. As we will soon explain, higher-priced mountain bikes have lighter stronger frames and better components that are made to withstand the tests of trends and trails. We think that just as important as what kind of bike you buy is where you buy it. Here's why.

You may think you are going to find a better deal by shopping at a discount or department store but, in the long run, you will probably end up paying more. First of all, you might be hard pressed to find anybody who can help you if you have any substantive questions, such as what the frame is made of and how, or its handling strengths and weaknesses. More importantly, though, after charging you an assembly fee, the department store clerks, not being trained bike mechanics, may make mistakes, or may leave parts of the preparation out of their routine to keep the assembly time per bike at a minimum. You will end up getting all the errors and shortcomings of the questionable assembly corrected at a real bike shop where expert attention is factored into the selling price of the bike. Since you cannot ride it until such problems are eliminated, the savings from a department store are deceptively thin.

Most bike shops offer limited free service on a new bike to get it "dialed in," to get the kinks out of the bike's performance after you have ridden it for a while. Spokes "settle" which requires minor truing, cables stretch and derailleurs may need a "tweak." Beyond that first free tuning, a shop may offer you longer term discounts on tune-ups, basic repairs or routine overhauls. (We will teach you how to keep these needs to a minimum in Chapter 12.) For subsequent repairs or service, the shop's sticker on your bike will likely get you preferential treatment — mechanics are prone to work on "their" bikes first.

As an added bonus, most bike shops offer discounts on accessories at the time you purchase a bike. This can mean substantial savings on helmets, shoes, bike bags, and water bottles — items that you will need regardless of where you get your bike.

And, despite what you may think, there are deals to be had at bike shops. If you can wait until mid-fall, you can save big bucks on that little number you saw in the spring. New bikes are previewed in September and dealers want to clear the showroom floor to make way for next year's hot ticket before the Christmas rush.

A bike from a good bike shop will be tuned up and sized just for you.

If you are far from the nearest shop or inclined to shop by mail order, there are several good national firms that sell bikes and equipment by phone. The obvious drawbacks are that you can't try out the bikes, will not be sure of size and fit, and will have to maintain the bike yourself or find a shop that will. If you buy a bike from a good shop, it will be tuned up and sized just for you and will probably get a free checkup after the break-in period. Bikes from a mail order firm come in a box with at least partial assembly required.

We think that it is definitely worth the extra miles you might have to drive to find a bike shop that will give you the quality, of both products and services, that you deserve.

Your Bike Size

As we mentioned in the last chapter, most mountain bikes in the past have been designed for a 180 pound male rider. Women, particularly those of smaller stature (for that matter, smaller men as well) have had difficulty finding properly sized and proportioned bikes. Things have recently changed and now, many manufacturers offer smaller models. However not all such bikes are well-conceived design-wise. When you keep the wheels the same size as the larger bikes (26 inches) and shrink the frame, subtle design changes take place.

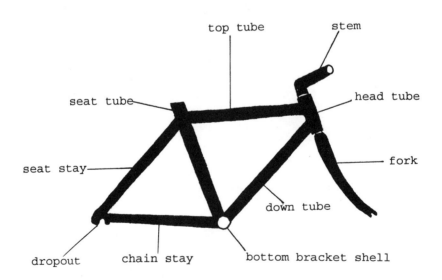

Not all shops carry smaller bikes so look for one that does. Try out some models and see how they feel. The one area that you can easily check is <u>standover height</u>. This is how you know if a bike is your "size" or not . And believe us, proper fit is important. Riding a bike that is too big is not only awkward on the trail, it can lead to a variety of back, leg, and knee injuries. Conversely, a bike that's too small is tricky to maneuver because your movements are confined, and proper adjustments such as seat height may not be safely possible.

Standover height is measured while you straddle the bike with both feet flat on the ground. The distance between your crotch and the top tube is the standover height. This distance should be a minimum of two inches. If, like most bikes, there is a slightly angled top tube, measure the distance using an imaginary horizontal line.

Why do some bikes have angled or sloping top tubes? Slightly lowering, and thereby lengthening, the top tube is believed to increase rigidity which benefits the bike's overall handling capabilities. Besides boosting the steering control, it also creates a larger, more maneuverable cockpit, the area between the seat and the handlebars where most of the power transfers from your shifting weight take place.

When you're looking at bikes, bear in mind that women are often attracted to bikes that are too small (and men seem to like them too big.) Using the two-inch rule, you can be certain that a bike is truly right for you.

So what does "bike size" really mean? The size is the vertical measurement of the distance between the top tube at a horizontal point and the bottom bracket, the part of the frame from which the pedals extend. Most bikes are available in sizes of 15 inches up to 21 inches. There are a handful of companies who have realized that a good portion of the consumer base, particularly women, may require smaller frames and now make available sizes all the way down to 12 inches.

The downside to many smaller-framed bikes is that the head tube (where the handlebar stem meets the frame) and the seat tube angles are not adjusted proportionately. This means that the stretch between the seat and the handlebar is more or less the same on a 14" bike as on a 21" bike. A lot of men might not notice this but women, traditionally shorter in torso than leg, will.

The good news is that there are several options now available to fine-tune the fit. The first and foremost option is this: you should get a bike that is proportionately sized. There are a couple on the market, and now that someone has addressed it, more manufacturers are sure to follow.

Second, buy a bike with a shorter handlebar stem extension. The average extension is 135 mm. You can get stems with extensions as short as 120 mm (with a 0, 10, or 20 degree rise, "rise" meaning the angle at which the handlebar sits, 0 being straight out) or some companies, for a price, will custom make them shorter. You can also get a touring stem which is a little bit taller with a dramatic rise but almost no extension. We don't recommend touring stems for serious off-road use, for they tend to throw off your balance on technical climbing and descending. A good bike shop will often find the right-sized stem hiding in the back room.

Your third option is to adjust your seat position. By moving the seat forward, you close the gap while improving your leverage. Your ideal seat position is easy to ascertain: with the pedals level, the bony protrusion below your forward knee should bisect your foot in a vertical line. If you want to measure it exactly, tie something heavy to a length of string while you, or a helper who can see your leg straight on, hold the loose end of the string against the bone. The heavy object should dangle near your instep, half the length of your foot.

Frame Materials

There are two primary factors that govern the price of a mountain bike: (a) the material composition from the frame, and (b) the components. We will get to the components in a minute.

Bike frames are constructed from one of five materials. In ascending price order, they are high-tensile steel, chromoly, aluminum, carbon fiber, and titanium. There are a couple of exotic alloy materials finding their way into bicycle manufacturing, hand-me-downs from the aerospace industry, but, so far, those are very big ticket items. For the purpose of discussion, we will stick to the five materials most commonly used.

Steel Frames

High-tensile steel is used only in low-end bikes, meaning bikes priced under $200. This is due to its excessive weight and inflexible nature. A straight-gauge steel frame rides like a tank, slow moving and difficult to maneuver.

A high-tensile steel frame.

Chromoly Frames

Chromoly, a lightweight steel alloy, is the popular material in the mid-range level, bikes priced between $300 to $800. Chromoly can be processed in varying strengths and weights, which are further enhanced by the tubes being butted at the joints, where strength is essential. "Butting" means that the walls of the frame

A mid-priced chromoly frame.

tubes, which are hollow, are thinner in the center and thicker by layer as they approach the ends. The majority of chromoly frames are double-butted, which means that, at a point near the joint, the walls get a little thicker and, closer still to the end, a little thicker than that. This allows the frame builder to make the walls in the center of the tube a little thinner, to save weight, without sacrificing strength. There are some high end bikes with chromoly frames which are triple-butted or have slightly oversized tubes which enables the frame builder to use thinner wall thicknesses.

The benefit of chromoly frames is their maneuvering flexibility. Generally speaking, chromoly bikes have a more active or compliant feel, particularly in technical situations. The downside, in some cases, is the somewhat heavier weight. We say "in some cases" because, depending on the make and performance model, the weights of chromoly bikes vary wildly, from low end clunkers to high end race-ready bikes almost as light as titanium.

Aluminum Frames

Aluminum is the frame material currently enjoying popularity with novice to pro racers, and those concerned with performance but who do not have the dollars or the desire to go all the way with titanium. Aluminum is strong, lighter than steel and made even lighter by larger diameter tubes with thinner wall thicknesses. The large diameter tubing is referred to as "blown out" or "oversized." Some frame builders utilize varying tube sizes within the same frame while others opt for the full oversized frame. Aside from its durable light weight, aluminum also has minor shock absorption capabilities. The frame itself will soften some of the rough spots which decreases rider fatigue. The flip side is one that may take getting used to, particularly to those coming from the chromoly experience: aluminum bikes are stiff, creating the illusion of an unforgiving or "heavy" ride. In our experience, that feeling goes away as you get accustomed to the sureness of the handling, often referred to as "point and shoot."

A high-end aluminum frame.

Carbon Fiber Frames

Carbon fiber has the same shock-absorbing characteristic as aluminum, although to a greater degree. Carbon fiber is, most simply put, high tech fiberglass — a netting-like material layered with a carbon composite shell.

There are two types of carbon fiber frames — lugged and molded. A lugged frame, which is usually less expensive, is one where the tubes in the main triangle are carbon fiber, pieced together by attaching the ends to aluminum, chromoly, and sometimes titanium joints, or lugs. The rear triangle is typically chromoly, which helps keep the price down. Molded frames, which are more expensive because of the special equipment required, are all one piece, formed with a mold either by injection (bladder molding) or a "clam-shell" (two sides bonded together).

Carbon fiber frames sit between aluminum and titanium in the lightweight category. Where aluminum feels stiffer than chromoly, carbon fiber feels more active. Due to its light weight and flexible nature, the compliance of the ride can be downright disconcerting until you get used to it. But again, the more time spent in the saddle, the more you can appreciate the responsiveness.

Both aluminum and carbon fiber bikes can be found priced as low as $700 and as high as $3000, depending on who makes the bike (there are only a handful of aluminum manufacturers who distribute or license their frames to a variety of bike companies), the brand of bike, and the components. To try to beat the cost, some people opt to purchase the frame by itself and outfit it with their old components and wheels, providing they fit. The fit can be a reality in some cases, or a wish. For example, if the rear axle spacing on your switched-over wheel is off, the freewheel cluster may not fit as well once the axle is reconfigured. If you are seriously considering this route, enlist the aid of your friendly mechanic to help out.

Titanium Frames

For the pièce de résistance, we now come to the reigning king of the hill, titanium. The feel of a well-built titanium bike can best be described as "plush." Like carbon fiber, it absorbs impact and like aluminum, it feels stiff and sure. And its light weight makes it extremely maneuverable.

Titanium is a naturally occurring, extremely lightweight and very strong metal. Titanium frames are most often sold on their own or as a frameset (frame and fork) because of the high cost. A frame alone is in the neighborhood of $1000 and up. The expertise required in processing titanium from mine shaft to bike tube factors greatly into the cost of this material. Its nature is such that a poorly constructed frame will bend or break under minimal pressure. Currently, the elite group of frame builders skilled in titanium frame manufacturing is very small. A well-built titanium frame dressed up with top-of-the-line components can run upwards of $5000. Kind of makes your mouth dry out, doesn't it?

Frames are meant to last a long time. Many bike shops will recommend that you buy a bike with the best frame that you can and later, as we describe in Chapter 11, upgrade to lighter and stronger components. Regardless of the frame material, as a woman you need to be at least a little concerned about a bike's overall weight. The lighter the bike, the easier it is to climb and to maneuver in technical sections, both uphill and downhill. Your bike should be light enough so that you, not the bike, dictate direction. While most men may be able to throw around and control a 27 to 30 pound bike, most women should look at bikes weighing 25 pounds or less. In the end, what your bike is made from and how it is made is up to you and your wallet.

Components

"Components", if you are unfamiliar with the term, are every part of the bike but the frame. At the heart of it, though, people are usually talking about the chainrings, shifters, derailleurs, rear cog set ("freewheel"), hubs, brakes and brake levers.

When you check out mountain bikes, you will find that each model has a specified component group. The higher priced the bike, the higher priced the components on the bike.

Pricing of components, both individually and as a group, is related to their degree of function, weight and durability. Low-end (economical) components are often a mix of plastic and steel, meant as a sort of starter kit. These parts allow you to get a feel for this whole mountain biking thing, but they will weigh you down and may not be up to the rigors of serious off-road riding. High-end (expensive) components, made up of an assortment of aluminum and titanium goodies, are often "race proven," having stood up to the abuses of pro racers through all types of rough and tumble conditions.

There is, of course, a happy middle ground: parts and accessories that may cost a little more but not so much that it will keep you awake at night. Mid-level components can be made of a variety of materials, mostly steel and chromoly, but you can find some inexpensive aluminum, as well. For the purposes of enthusiasts or enthusiasts-to-be, mid-range groups are a good place to start. You will find these on bikes priced in the $600 to $800 dollar range. High performance groups are generally reserved for the higher end bike frames, in the $850 to $1200 and beyond category.

Most components are available aftermarket, for those with an eye towards future upgrading. In other words, bike shops and mail order houses sell the component parts separately for you to upgrade in stages. One manufacturer distributes components by performance group, wherein the various parts can only be replaced with an identical part. Parts from this company are priced according to group. If you want to upgrade one part, you have to replace everything. Other manufacturers allow more room for mixing and matching, either within their own lines or with another manufacturer's, to permit true customizing.

When you are comparison shopping for bikes, the one component that stands out with a "Why are these different and which is better?" question attached are shifters. There are three types of shifters available - thumb shifters (mounted on top of the handlebar), trigger shifters (mounted below the handlebar), and twist shifters (that look like they are part of the grips).

Thumb shifters came first. They were the industry standard until one of the big component manufacturers attempted to "improve" on the concept, which really meant that they wanted to set

Thumbshifters

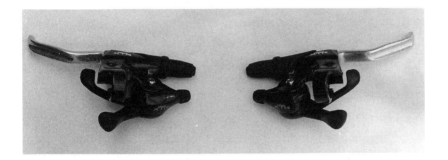

Trigger Shifters

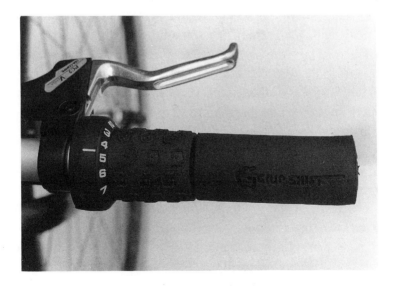

Twist Shifters

themselves apart, flood the market, and create a new standard. Enter the trigger shifter. Not long thereafter came another upstart to shake things up, translating the motorcycle throttle idea to mountain biking — the evolution of the twist shifter.

Why are there three types of shifters? Simple: competition. Bicycle componentry is a lucrative market, evidenced by the dramatically increased mountain bike sales over the last several years. Products that make it to the level of acceptance by the general riding public can revolutionize the industry, not to mention make a mint for the manufacturer.

Which is better? It all boils down to individual preference. You will find people who vehemently love each of these shifters, and an equal number who vehemently do not. The question is not which one is better but rather which one feels most comfortable to use. Test ride them all. You will soon discover which one suits you.

Saddles

There is a common myth in cycling which says: women require oversize bicycle seats. This just ain't so. It's a personal fit. Each of our bodies is different, therefore no one can say patently what is right for each of us. Some women (and men) prefer the comfort of larger saddles while others go for the performance characteristics of small seats. Still others like something medium-sized.

The basis for the big seat contention is simple: as a beginner, you get saddle sore. Most women are willing to accept that their legs will be sore, or their arms, or both, but some women had not thought about the fact that their rears or their crotch would be sore. We are not talking about excruiating pain but rather some discomfort and perhaps a little stiffness, akin to, although certainly less than, one might experience after riding a horse for the first time (and look at the size of those saddles).

The truth of the matter is, for most women whom we have spoken with, the soreness goes away, as it does in the rest of their bodies, exponentially to the amount of time spent riding. Your entire body needs time to adjust. The more you ride, the better you can truly judge what saddle size is right for you.

There is something which you can do to make the breaking-in period (as we call it) more pleasant. Start off with a mid-sized saddle, perhaps even a saddle with gel-like implants. As your riding time increases and your riding style becomes more defined, either swap seats with someone you ride with to see how their saddle feels or check your local bike shop and try something new. (Check for sales.) This is the approach that we both took and now we each have three saddles. We have kept them all so that we can change our seats from small performance saddles that we usually ride to a larger saddle for road riding or touring. (Never throw away spare bike parts; you may have times you wish you had them back.)

Many saddle manufacturers make "women's" models which are a little shorter and anywhere from a little to a lot wider than regular saddles. The extended width purports to increase support to a woman's pelvic region. Some of them also have cut-outs or perforations in the saddle shell. (You can see these when you turn the saddle upside down.) These indentations, when coupled with the shorter saddle nose, are designed to alleviate some of the pressure on the contact points, aptly called "pressure points."

The drawback to most of these types of saddles is that the width impairs off-the-saddle maneuvering (which we will be covering later). The good news is that there is at least one saddle that meets this challenge, the Terry Precision ATB Women's saddle. Like other types of women's saddles, it is a little shorter and a little wider than regular saddles but it is small enough to not prohibit movement. Hopefully, more manufacturers will follow suit.

If you happen to feel real "hey-this-really-hurts" pain in your hips or pelvis when riding, don't automatically blame it on the saddle. There is a feature of bicycles known as the "Q factor" which is the measurement between the two pedals — thus the distance between your feet when riding. This distance is fairly standardized on most bikes but some women find that distance too narrow, which means that their feet are too close together, forcing their legs into a bow-legged riding position. This will result in pain in the hips or pelvis. If you should experience this kind of pain, the Q factor is the likely offender.

To handle this problem, stop by your bike shop and order pedal spindle extensions (larger bike shops may stock them but the smaller ones generally do not). These are spacers which fit between the pedal and the crank arm and, by moving the pedals farther out, increase the width between your feet. This alleviates the strain to the pelvic region.

As we said earlier, you'll be a little sore, regardless of the type of saddle you buy, until you ride yourself into shape. Find a saddle that you like and don't worry, the discomfort will vanish after just a few rides.

Pedals

These days, just about everyone uses some form of foot binding on their pedals. There are two reasons for you to join their ranks. Reason One: with your feet locked to your pedals, there are no wasted motions; while one foot is pushing, the other one is pulling, at all times. You will most appreciably notice this benefit while climbing. Reason Two is obvious: the binding device prevents your feet from flying off the pedals at inopportune moments, like, say on a particularly bumpy downhill.

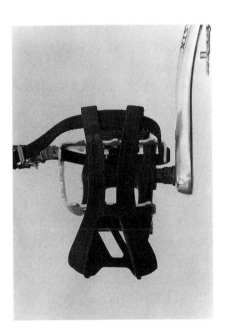

Toe Clip

The choices in pedal bindings are toe clips, pedal straps, and "clipless" pedals.

A toe clip is actually a plastic cage for the toe of your shoe which tightens, with a strap, across the widest part of your foot. The tighter the strap, the less play your foot is allowed, i.e., movement while in the clip and ease of moving in and out. Although you may not notice it, you steer your bike with your whole body, feet included. Therefore, your feet need a small amount of room to move while in the toe clips. The fit should be snug but not tight. And in the interest of safety, you should be able to move your feet in and out with a reasonable degree of freedom. If an effort is required to release your foot, it is too tight.

Pedal straps, such as Power Grips™, are a lot like stirrups. You slip your foot in at a slight angle and straighten your foot to tighten the hold. The tighter the strap, the firmer the lock between your foot and the pedal. These allow for more foot movement while in the straps. Again, make sure you can move in and out of them somewhat freely.

Clipless pedals require special shoes as the pedal actually locks onto the bottom of the shoe. Different brands lock on in different ways but generally, they lock and release with a sharp movement at a certain angle. There is usually an adjustable amount of float, or free movement, while locked on. If you get clipless pedals, practice the release movement over and over, before you ever hit a trail. We suggest practicing on soft ground such as grass, to prevent any damage if you tip over. The motion should be second nature.

Water Bottles

When you are looking at new bikes, note the number of water bottle cage mounts. Just about all mountain bikes are equipped with at least one. Those from forward-thinking manufacturers come with two (or three). Water cage mounts will appear on the down tube (the lower tube of the front, main triangle) and/or on the seat tube (the "vertical" tube that holds the seat post) as a pair of allen-head bolts, a couple of inches apart, that are just kind of there, not really doing anything.

To mount a water cage, which is usually sold separately, you simply remove the bolts, match up the holes on the backing of the cage with the holes in the bike frame, and put the bolts back.

If your bike has only one mount and you decide to be smart and carry a second bottle, under no circumstances should you or anyone else attempt to drill out holes in your frame. You will compromise your frame's strength and probably nullify any warranties or guarantees. You can get a mounting bracket kit at any bike shop which consists of a pair of metal bands and a couple of nuts and bolts. You slip the bands over the back of the cage and tighten them down around the frame tube.

Since most pre-drilled cage mounts are on the down tube, the logical place to mount a second cage is on the seat tube. When deciding on the placement of the cage, make sure you allow full clearance for the front derailleur operation while allowing enough room for a large, 27 ounce bottle.

So, now you have a bike, you have your water bottles, and you are ready to roll, right? Well, not just yet. There is one more piece of required equipment for all bicyclists: a helmet.

Helmets

Eighty-five percent of the injuries sustained on bicycles, on and off-road, are preventable by wearing a helmet. Aside from the obvious safety factor, a helmet is good for your psyche. A lot of the finesse needed for a pleasant dirt-filled experience comes from a good mental attitude. A helmet does wonders for your confidence and morale.

This is another item which you should purchase only at a bike shop. Why? Because, while there is no law (yet) governing the safety regulations of bike helmets, there are two generally accepted quality standards, the ANSI and Snell certifications. You'll find a sticker, both inside the helmet and on the box, indicating that a prototype helmet passed their respective impact tests and met one or both of the approval standards.

As these safety-tested helmets are of a necessarily high quality, the prices can be outside the target range for a lot of discounters or department stores. While you could spend upwards of $100, the median price is under $50. And, unless otherwise specified by the manufacturer (although we cannot think of one exception), the helmets are guaranteed for life. If you ever fall and your helmet's integrity is at all impacted, you simply ship it back to the manufacturer and, for a nominal fee which varies by brand, they will send you a new one. Or, take it back to your local bike shop and they'll replace it for you right there and then if you bought the helmet there. This is another reason to deal with a shop and not just any store.

How do you find the right helmet? Once you've found one that meets the fore-mentioned standards, your primary concern is fit — a helmet is useless if it doesn't fit properly. All good manufacturers let you to personalize the size by including strips of foam rubber that to attach to the inside of the helmet with either Velcro™ or glue backing. The helmet should fit the top of your head like a glove.

The next consideration is ventilation. That's what those long cutouts are for. Remember, your head and feet are the trapping

The unsafe "jaunty" look.

The proper helmet fit

zones for body heat. Even on a cold day, you're likely to work up a sweat on a mountain bike. The more heat that is allowed to escape, the more comfortable you'll be. Make sure that you choose a helmet that allows for suitable air flow.

Beyond these points, it's simply a matter of taste. Helmets come in a wide variety of color schemes and styles. Some offer aerodynamic shapes, more head coverage, less head coverage, visors, and so on. Try a few on and see how you like them.

After you have made the purchase, have all the pads in place, and are raring to go, the final step is to adjust the straps properly. You're not looking for the "jaunty" or "casual" look — that helmet is there to protect your head. It can't do that if it is slipping off the back of your head or if it flies off in a spill. The straps should be adjusted tight enough so that you can not get a finger in between the strap and your chin — so tight that you have to release your chin strap to eat. Your helmet may be called upon one day for active duty — you don't want it falling down on the job.

Other Accessories

So, now you have the bike, have the water, are sporting the latest helmet style and are off, right? You are just about there. In the interest of preparedness and to ensure your riding enjoyment, unmarred by cries of "I'm hungry" or "I thought you had your wallet," we recommend carrying a bike bag.

Our personal favorite is the under-the-saddle bag. They attach to the seat post and the rails in your saddle, handy yet out of your way. Any weight added to the bike due to its contents goes largely unnoticed as it is in the same general area as your center of gravity. They come in a variety of sizes and are designed to hold such necessities as wallets, money, keys, and trailside snacks.

There is another, triangle-shaped bike bag that attaches to bike frames at points within the main triangle. If this style strikes your fancy, take your bike bag-shopping with you to be certain that a triangle bag will fit properly. Frames with a sloping top tube have different shape requirements than those with a horizontal top tube; a triangle bag may not fit.

You also need to consider the type of riding you do or will do. Will there be occasions when you will need to carry ("portage") your bike over unsteady or impassable terrain? If so, a triangle bag might get in the way. We have seen the type of triangle bag with the shoulder brace built into it and we have tried it. Unfortunately, it made portaging more difficult as the bag just happened to attach at the balance point which made hand placement a problem. If your bike frame is 18 inches or larger, you might not have the same problem we, with our 16 inch frames, did. On the positive side, a triangle bag is more accessible while you're riding. You don't need to stop or get off the bike to rifle through it.

Your third bag option is a handlebar bag. It is sort of an update of the basket idea. You get the benefit of accessibility without the bag getting in the way, provided, of course, that it is not crimping your shift or brake cables. It will add weight to the front end which may impair steering control, in the case of one who does not believe in traveling light. We have never used a handlebar bag but we have a friend who swears by them.

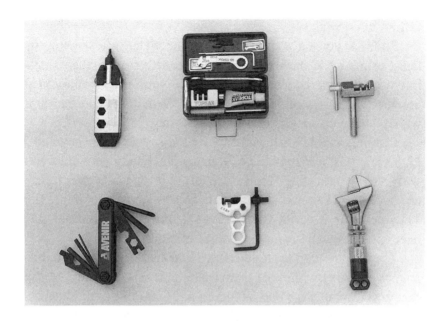

An assortment of multi-tools.

There are a handful of items that you should keep in your bike bag, regardless of style, at all times: a chain breaker, 4 mm, 5 mm and 6 mm allen wrenches (the three standard sizes for bike components and accessories), a small adjustable wrench, and a spoke wrench. Also, bring some quarters for a phone call. You never know when you might need one or more of these things and, believe us, you do not want to be caught needing something that you left in the car twenty miles away. We'll be teaching you how to use some of these things in Chapter 12.

There are several "multi-tools" available — pocket or bike bag-sized contraptions comprised of a few or all of the above items. They give you a compact and relatively lightweight way to be prepared. Another alternative of which we are aware is a miniature tool box which includes scaled down versions of the most frequently used items. The box is roughly the size of a deck of cards (although a little shorter and a little deeper) and can fit comfortably in most bike bags.

Rounding out the list of necessities are tire tools, a patch kit, a spare inner tube, an adhesive bandage or two, and a form of tire inflation, be it compressed air cartridges or a pump. It's also a good idea to carry a photocopy of your driver's license or identification card with a copy of your health insurance card or information. When you start riding with some frequency, you will learn your own needs, if any, beyond these essentials.

As you get ready to hit the trail, we turn your attention to what to wear. First of all, eye protection is a must in mountain biking. Aside from the glare on sunny days, it is smart to protect the eyes from foreign matter. Mountain bike tires pick up and toss a lot of dirt and pebbles and in the woods, small branches can whip across your face before you see them. Whether you lean toward the racy iridescent model or a more conventional set of sunglasses, always wear eye protection when riding off-road.

Now, let's talk about lycra. We are well aware that most beginners have an aversion to bike shorts. We did, too. They look funny and they feel funny. That is, until you have spent an entire afternoon on a bike saddle. Bike shorts and bike pants have a padded crotch; the pad configurations are slightly different for women than men to achieve the most comfort possible. But why do they have to be so tight? Actually, while they look tight, bike shorts are quite comfortable. And the "second skin" design serves two purposes. First, as we will be discussing in the next few chapters, mountain bike riding requires a lot of moving around. Bike shorts won't bunch up, thus preventing chafing. The second reason will be apparent the first time you shift your weight back — bike shorts won't get hung up on the nose of the saddle. Once you've given them a try, you too will be a convert.

Gloves are another item worn by most cyclists. Cycling gloves have padded palms and can help assure more hours of comfortable riding. They come with various finger lengths, from fingerless to full gloves. In the spring and summer, the choice is yours but for winter riding, full gloves are a must. Talk to your bike shop friends for hints on the best gear to wear for your part of the country.

"(Mountain biking) is one of the most challenging and fun things I've ever had a chance to do."

Susan DeMattei
Top-ranking professional cross-country racer
Diamond Back Racing Team

Chapter 3

Riding on the Level

Now we get to the fun part. In the next three chapters, we'll explain those little mysteries of technique, or how to do the stuff that other people make look so easy. We'll start with the basics of riding on level ground, then we will move on to climbing, and, saving the best for last, downhilling.

Proper Seat Height

First things first. You need to know the proper height placement of your seat. Proper seat height is crucial to your performance; not only because of the power transferred by the most effective use of leverage but because, if your seat isn't at the correct height, after a few miles you'll be in pain. Your knees will hurt, your back will hurt, or both. Riding with your seat too high or too low for a prolonged period, say a few months, may result in serious, perhaps permanent, damage. In the interest of your own well being, make sure your seat is adjusted properly to your height.

You would not believe how many variations people will give you when you ask for their advice on this. Unfortunately, most of it is wrong. The bad advice runs the gamut of "in a horizontal line with your handlebars, three inches above your handlebars, knees bent at the bottom stroke, legs straight on the bottom stroke," and so on. Here's some good advice.

Proper seat height.

We've surveyed and experimented, talked to racers and recreational riders, seen it all, heard it all. Write this one in stone: With a pedal all the way down at the bottom of the rotation, place your foot so that the back of your heel is flush with the back of the pedal. (See photo on facing page.) Your seat should be placed high enough that your leg is almost, but not quite, straight. Do not allow your knees to lock. Regardless of what people try to tell you, there is no correct seat height that can be determined by inches as all legs are not created equal in length.

And since we're talking about seats, have you ever wondered why it's nearer to the rear wheel than the front? The reason, as you may have guessed, is traction. The bicycle is a rear-wheel drive, front controlled vehicle. The rear wheel gets you going while the front wheel points out the way. You're actually pushing yourself forward as opposed to pulling. That's why the drivetrain is coupled with the rear wheel. And that's why traction is your best friend on the trail.

Pedalling Efficiently

To get that traction, you first need to know how to pedal efficiently. Everyone who has ever ridden a bike as a kid knows how to make the pedals move. But not everyone knows how to move them with the most strength and the least effort. There are a few simple tricks to it. The first one is form: bend your knees in, almost letting them touch the top tube. If you make contact once in a while, you're doing it right. If you make contact constantly, you're being overzealous. Back off a bit.

Keeping your knees in promotes the most power to the pedal with the least amount of wear and tear on your joints. Pedalling with your knees out is unnecessarily rough on your legs because all the force and effort is coming directly from them. With your knees together, the real oomph is coming not only from your quads, which is the primary source of power, but also from your abs, that underrated but no less powerful muscle group. The abdominal muscles are among the strongest in your body. Pedalling from the gut harnesses that energy.

Make a complete pedal stroke.

In your travels, you may have noticed people riding who look like they're stomping their pedals. This is exactly what not to do. This is yet another way to injure your all-too-delicate knees. Not to mention a waste of effort. Which brings us to pedalling trick number two: a complete pedal stroke. Efficient pedalling involves constant motion. While one leg is pushing, make the other leg pull to round out the stroke. As you push down the right pedal, lift your left foot. This "pulls" the left pedal which reduces the amount of effort required to push the right pedal. This way, you get twice the power using half the energy.

Viewing yourself as the engine of your bike, your legs are logically like the pistons. If you look closely at pistons in action, you'll see an arm attached to the bottom and notice that it is not actually moving up and down but in a circular motion that pushes the piston up at the top of the rotation. Your pedals are not unlike those swingarms.

All the motions in your bike's drivetrain are more or less circular. Your pedals move in a circle which moves the chainrings in a circle which moves the chain in a circle which pulls the gears in a circle to make your back wheel move in a circle which makes your front wheel move in a circle. Making the best use of your efforts in this sea of circles is simply a matter of paying attention to the rotation rhythm. This is the third trick; it's called cadence.

Some people keep track of their cadence by counting, either mentally or electronically, their rpms or rotations per minute. This seems a little too literal to us and like way too much trouble. Our preferred method is to stay in tune with the rhythm of the movement itself. Find a comfortable, steady pace and keep to it, shifting up and down as necessary to maintain the rhythm.

Shifting

In addition to pumping the pedals, knowing how and when to shift plays an equally important role. We'll go over "when" a little later. The "how" is one of those things that everyone takes for granted that you know; of course, you don't know if nobody tells you. So we will.

You shift down, into an easier gear, for climbing.

Whether you have trigger or twist shifters, the principle is the same. The left shifter controls the front derailleur. You have three position ("ring") choices corresponding to the three chainrings. Shifting up will make pedalling harder, shifting down will make it easier. The right shifter controls the rear derailleur. Here, you have either seven or eight choices ("gears"), depending on the component package. Again, shifting up will make pedalling harder, shifting down will make it easier. Thumb shifters are slightly different. Moving the left lever up will make pedalling harder, moving it down will make it easier, just like the other shifters. But the right lever is opposite — shifting up will make it easier to pedal, shifting down will make it harder.

Now, all this "up" and "down" talk can get very confusing when you are talking about shifting the gears. Everyone seems to mean something different. Two of the shift lever manufacturers have even resorted to numbering the gears on the lever/shift unit indicators. In keeping with their system and to clarify our position here, when we say "down" or "low" we mean easier gears; when we say "up" or "high," we mean harder gears.

You may have seen a bike mechanic spin your rear wheel, running your chain and derailleurs up and down the spectrum while testing the shifters for smoothness and adjustment. To see the effects of shifting for yourself, while you are dismounted, have a friend grab the frame or seat post and hold the back wheel off the ground while you turn the pedal forward with one hand. As you are turning the pedal, with your other hand zip through all the different gears and combinations, using both shifters. This is the best way to illustrate exactly what the derailleurs do while feeling the chain tension change as the chain hops from gear to gear.

We all know why you would want pedalling to be easier but why would you want to make it harder? When the pedal stroke is "harder," it means you're in a larger gear ratio (chainring to rear cog.) The larger the gear ratio, the more ground you cover with each pedal stroke. This is how you go faster. This doesn't mean that you should try to ride in your biggest gear all the time to go fast. Speed (not to mention control) is dictated by pedalling efficiently. When you feel your chain getting slack (pedalling gets easier in your present gear), shifting up one gear will increase the tension, thus keeping your pedal stroke even. Conversely, if pedalling becomes too difficult and you are really having to push (watch those knees!), shifting down will ease the tension, both to the chain and your legs.

Riding Technique

Now that you are armed with a proper seat adjustment and a rudimentary understanding of shifting, let's hit the road for a little practice. That's right, "road" — preferably a smooth dirt road, or low-traffic pavement, especially if it has been a while (years) since you have ridden. (If you are comfortable riding already, skip ahead to the next chapter.) The smooth pavement makes it easier to work on technique and build up the confidence before working your way on to grass and then trails. School parking lots on weekends are great places to practice; find a place that works for you and let's mount up.

Start off in a medium gear, with the chain on the middle ring on the front and somewhere in the middle or larger ring on the rear. You may want to skip the toe clips until you've put in some time on the bike. If you have them, get a pedal in the ten o'clock position, slip your foot in one clip, and hop on, starting to pedal as you do. Grasp the handle grips lightly and keep your arms and upper body relaxed. The key to balance is staying loose. Pedal smoothly and give the brakes a try.

Oh yes, the left lever is for the front brake. Apply that one judiciously. The right lever controls the rear brakes. Use the brakes together, rear first, then front — as you practice, work at slowing down smoothly.

We will teach you some riding refinements later on but for now, you want to get accustomed to the feel of the bike. The more you ride, the easier balance and turning become.

Turns are accomplished as much with your body as the front wheel. As you ride along, practice leaning yourself and your bike in the direction you want to turn. It will feel a little disconcerting at first — just relax as much as possible. If you need help convincing

When riding on grass, stay loose and let the bike handle the bumps.

your body to lean, stick an elbow out in the same direction as the turn. Work on turns remembering, as you get rolling faster, that you want to brake as you approach the turn, just as in a car. "Slow in, fast out" as Cathy's dad always said.

Graduate to grass or dirt. Here is where the confidence you built will pay off. Stay loose and let the bike handle the bumps and the undulations — that is what it was designed to do. You will find that you have to be in an easier gear when off the pavement due to the higher rolling resistance. Stay on the smallest front ring for most grass riding practice.

Trail and dirt road riding is what mountain biking is all about. Find some gently rolling terrain and practice what you have learned. Experiment with the different gear combinations. Mountain bikes have a minimum of 21 gears, some have 24. Practice shifting until you can identify how each of those gears feels. The goal is to be so adept at shifting, you can do it without thinking.

Once you have the shifting down pat, work on using the gears to maintain a steady cadence. Some trails, like rolling singletrack, call for frequent gear changes to keep the cadence consistent. Feel free to shift as often as you like; there is no such thing as shifting too much. After some pedalling on a rolling track, you'll find a cadence or rhythm that feels good where you are not pushing too hard or spinning your pedals too fast. It's just right. You have found that level where you're a riding machine. Then, looming ominously ahead, is a hill. Kind of a steep thing.

No problem. Keep reading the next few pages and we'll climb a mountain together .

"Make sure you always have fun and don't feel pressure to overcome every obstacle; that will come in time. Meanwhile, you have your good days and you have your bad days."

Jan Bolland
Professional racer
Team Evian

Chapter 4

Climbing

Mountain bikes are born to climb. All it takes to conquer hills that you never thought possible is a little conditioning, a little anticipation, a little technique, and a lot of practice. You can ride a chairlift to the top of some mountains and ride jeeps to the summits of others. We think that the downhill run, aka the payoff, is a lot sweeter when you earn it the old fashioned way, by pedaling to the top of the hill.

Getting Legs and Lungs Ready

You need to be in condition to tackle any serious climbs on a mountain bike but the great thing is, you can get both your lungs and your legs in shape by getting out and riding, starting first on some small hills and gradually working your way up longer and steeper climbs. Climbing builds muscles and aerobic capacity. Along with the obvious gains in your leg strength, you'll also gradually acquire more upper body strength from holding yourself up while keeping the bike under control. You also can get a heck of a workout for your cardiovascular system. By riding hills frequently, your lungs, not unlike a muscle, get stronger and their capacity increases. At first,

Anticipate the hill. Shift down before starting up.

you will huff and puff like you are trying to blow out a fire in the next county but pretty soon, your breathing becomes easier as your aerobic capacity grows.

You should probably think about working on your leg strength off the bike as well. As you build up your legs, your out-of-the-saddle mobility increases and you can harness that traction action from all different points.

A good way to work on your legs, not to mention your lung capacity, is to take stairs up at every available opportunity. Start gradually. Start off by walking up escalators. Where there are escalators, there are usually stairs. Graduate to walking up these, then trotting. If you don't encounter stairs on a regular basis, visit your local high school and jog up the stands in the playing field.

You may notice that we keep stressing "up." This is because going down stairs can be hard on your knees. The point is to build up your quads, not grind down your tendons. So whether you climb hills, stairs, or bleachers, run up and then walk down.

Anticipating The Hill

One of the keys to climbing — and mountain bike riding in general for that matter — is anticipating, planning your moves ahead of time. When starting a climb, you want to be in the correct gear as you hit the first rise, and that takes anticipation.

See that hill ahead? Let's go for it. We'll start with the left shifter. As you are cruising along, you are probably in the middle chainring on the front. To get up most hills with a reasonable degree of ease, you should shift down to the small chainring ("granny gear") before you start up. Keep your pedal cadence steady and as you begin the climb, shift down a click or two with your right shifter to keep your pedals spinning. It is better to shift too early than wait too long but we will get to that in a moment. First, let's get up that hill. Here's how.

Climbing Technique

Technique, particularly body position, plays a big role in climbing. With the seat back on the rear end of the bike, your center of gravity is right about the location of your abdomen, with the majority of your weight digging the back tire in. By putting your hands on the handlebar, you're evenly distributing your weight between the front and back so that your front tire doesn't fly up nor does your back wheel spin. With proper traction, your tires do most of the work for you. The secret to effective climbing is keeping that traction centered — if you are too far forward, the weight goes off the back wheel and traction is lost. Conversely, if you sit too upright, you can accidentally "pop a wheelie." It takes a little saddle time to read the grade since each hill is different. But the more you ride, the better your feel for the proper climbing position.

Stay seated for moderate climbs

Basically, climbing can be accomplished by one of two methods: seated or "out of the saddle." For slight to moderate grades, you should stay seated. Keep a loose grip on the handlebars and lean forward, keeping your back flat and your weight balanced, putting more weight on the front tire without sacrificing rear tire traction. The steeper the hill, the more you need to lean. At the same time, bend your arms, tucking your elbows in against your body. This relieves tension in your chest and enables you to continue to breath deeply and steadily while climbing. Another helpful hint is to gently pull back on the handlebar — this increases your leverage which, in turn, increases your strength. Above all, keep your pedals moving, shifting as often as needed.

For moderate to downright steep inclines, you may need the extra leverage achieved by raising your body out of the saddle and

"Get up on the pedals" to climb steeper sections.

moving slightly forward. "Getting up on the pedals" is not only a good way to climb the steeper sections, it also can be a nice change of pace in a longer climb. Most experienced riders climb seated, then get up and forward for a bit, then transition back to the seat.

In either method, the position of your body should correspond to the grade. If the back tire slips or gets a little overactive on you, you're too far forward. If your front tire slips or you are all over the trail, you are too far back.

Don't get discouraged if you fail to get up out of the saddle at first. Like the punch line to the old joke about getting to Carnegie Hall, practice, practice, practice. Beginners have been known to plop right down as if they were pushed. If this happens, just lean forward to make the most of the seated position. And try again.

You can practice standing up while riding on level ground by shifting to tougher gears. Get on the middle chainring in front and shift to a gear that is not too hard. (Pushing gears that are too hard for too long leads to a variety of knee injuries.) Get up on the pedals and try to stay up for a couple of minutes at a time. Shift to an easier gear as you sit down and in a few moments, try it again. As you get the motion down pat with the hard gears and feel comfortable, find an easy climb and try out the technique.

A simple strategy is required for long, steep climbs. Keep your cadence as steady as you can. Push a gear that's as easy as possible, relax, and take it slow. Trying to climb a long trail too fast will burn out your muscles before you even make it halfway; you'll end up pushing your bike to the top. Remember the tortoise and the hare. By keeping your speed down, you'll make it uphill faster and more effectively than you would trying to race exhaustion.

There is an advanced climbing method that's favored by some of the top cross-country racers. It's something you have to work up to as it requires a little more strength and balance. As you're pedalling out of the saddle, rock slightly with the pedal stroke; back on the down stroke, forward on the upstroke. This little maneuver takes a lot of practice to avoid exaggerating the motion.

There will always be times when "push comes to shove." If the hill is just too steep, hop off and push the bike up the hill. If your quads are burning on a long climb, get off and push for a while, using different leg muscle groups, and then get back on and climb.

As we said earlier, you want to be able to anticipate your gearing needs before you find yourself attempting to grind a high gear on a steep grade. Shifting a moment or two early ensures a smooth, trouble-free transition. As you approach and start the climb, shift down once or twice when necessary to keep the rhythm steady. It gets a little steeper. Shift down again and get up off the seat. As it levels off, shift up and sit down. It starts to slope downhill a little. Shift up again. Click, click, click.

Shifting too late for a climb, or "shifting under pressure," puts undue tension on your chain and derailleurs, causing very unkind noises to come from the rear of your bike. It can also give you first-hand experience with chain suck and thrown chains.

"Chain suck" is the term for the chain doubling back on itself, mid-gear change, and getting jammed, either between the chain-rings or between the crank and the frame. You can pry the chain out by hand or with that small screwdriver you keep in your bag.

Once your chain has sucked, get it replaced. Few are the chains which don't get bent or twisted in the sucking process.

"Throwing the chain" means that the chain wasn't quite ready for you to change chainrings so it flies off all of them, landing around the bottom bracket. To put the chain back on the chainring, move the left shift lever to the bottom (low) position, roll the bike forward and place the chain on the little ring by hand.

Everyone throws a chain once in a while. If it happens more than a couple of times, though, it's time for a new chain or a derailleur adjustment.

Once you fully master the technique of climbing, you'll learn a secret: climbing is easier than most people think. It's simply a matter of getting some conditioning, learning how to stay one or two steps ahead of the bike, and keeping a steady rhythm up the hill. Much like the beat of life, rhythm plays a large and important role in climbing. From rhythm comes grace and agility.

"Courage is the price that life exacts for granting peace."

Amelia Earhart
Courage

Chapter 5

Downhill

The most exhilarating and rewarding aspect of off-road riding, for most people, is the downhill. As we mentioned in the last chapter, it's the payoff, the reason you worked so hard to get to the top of the mountain. There is an undeniable feeling of soul-stirring abandon in the moment that you give yourself over to the descent. And the sense of pride and empowerment experienced upon triumphing over fear is unmatchable.

Downhill trails come in a variety of shapes and sizes. There are fire roads, singletracks, rock faces and drop-offs, just to name a few. Some trails are almost as smooth as pavement while others may be little more than some dust thrown on top of a bunch of rocks and tree roots.

The challenges faced by a mountain biker, in these and other downhill situations, are comprised of equal parts psychological determination and physical agility. For this reason, downhill riding is the most demanding facet of mountain biking.

What surprises a lot of beginners and non-mountain bike riders are the physical benefits gained by downhilling. Using the proper out-of-the-saddle technique, a downhill run works your calves, quads, hips, abs, shoulders, triceps, biceps, lats, and pecs. It also builds and refines balance, coordination, and reflexes. The more rugged the trail, the harder the workout. If you're in it strictly for the exercise, what more could you possibly ask?

For those of us who are in it for the fun, the pupil-dilating, heart-gyrating, adrenaline-circulating, soul-liberating benefits are just as rewarding.

Know Your Brakes

But before we send you trundling off down a mountain, you need to know a bit more about your brakes. Your brakes are at your disposal to slow you down, stop you, and give you a hand at steering at cruising speed.

Look closely and you will notice the cables leading out of your brake lever housing. Following the cables, you will find that the right brake cable leads to your rear wheel, the left cable to the front wheel. As you depress the brake, the lever pulls on the cable, shortening it. This pulls the other end of the cable that's attached to the cantilever straddle cable or the horseshoe brake cable pull which closes the gap between the brake shoe and the wheel rim.

The rear brake is primarily a coaster brake. It won't bring you to a full and complete stop unless you're moving fairly slowly on level ground. Its primary purpose is to help you keep your speed manageable as you feather or modulate the brake lever (applying occasional light pressure.) Avoid locking this brake up, i.e., abruptly or continuously squeezing it as hard as you can. This will cause the rear end of the bike to swing out in response to the sudden loss of traction. This is how you slide, which some people, particularly racers, will do on purpose to bomb in and out of a turn quickly.

If you start to slide unintentionally, steer into it like you do in a car. Loosen up on the brake, turn your handlebars in the direction of the slide and you will right yourself.

The front brake is your stopping power. Never, never, never use the front brake alone. Think about what happens when you are walking behind someone who suddenly stops. Because you're still moving, you run right into them. The same principle applies to your

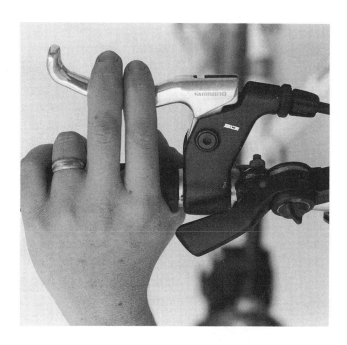

The front brake is powerful. Use light pressure on the brake lever.

wheels. When the front wheel stops independently of the rear wheel, the rear wheel doesn't get the message so it keeps on going. You can literally flip right off the seat and over the handlebars. That's called an instant endo.

The brakes are meant to be used as a pair, 50/50, whenever you want to stop. The rear brake slows down the action, adding light pressure from the front brake slows you down even more, evenly distributed pressure fore and aft will stop you. Feel free to use a little more back brake, if you like.

If you are the type who favors riding in full-on conditions (foul weather), it would be wise to swap your multi-purpose brake pads for those made expressly for wet riding. Standard brake pads are okay in most cases, but they tend to slip and make unnerving noises when they are wet or excessively muddy. When your favorite trail resembles a waterfall, there's a lot to be said for positive braking performance.

Downhill Technique

Whether you ride in summer or winter, down gentle slopes, fast, sweeping fire roads, or short technical drop-offs, the basic technique is the same. The first thing you need to do is level your pedals, meaning put them both at the halfway point where they are parallel to the ground (or at 3 o'clock and 9 o'clock if you prefer), and lift yourself slightly off the saddle. Level pedals are less likely to catch on any underbrush, tall roots, rocks, or the edges of deep ruts.

The next step is to place your body in the best leverage position. Your body position depends on the degree of the descent. Start off with your backside hovering slightly back from your regular seated position, knees bent, arms loose, your thighs resting on or lightly gripping the wings of your saddle. This way, your gluteous maximus puts a little more traction over the back tire, where it belongs. It also increases your rear braking strength. The steeper the trail, the further back you go.

Body position for a gradual downhill.

Keeping yourself off the seat this way while keeping your back flat saves you from undue wear and tear and gives you maximum control. Use your legs like shock absorbers. Downhill control is a matter of active leverage and balance which are sometimes more difficult to achieve when you are sitting down. The more active the terrain, the more active the rider should be.

Body position for a steep downhill.

Avoid standing straight up. While it is fun to do on an easy downslope, the pogo stance is worse for your control than staying glued to the saddle. The lower your center of gravity, the easier it is to control your bike, especially on long or technical descents. You may consider taking a moment to lower your seat before you begin to encourage yourself to stay low. Just remember to reset it at the correct height when you reach the bottom.

The variation of the standard downhill position comes when taking a turn. Unless you found a trail that goes straight up and straight down, you'll need to turn. The secret to effectively mastering turns, both at high speeds and low, is to drop your outside foot to the bottom of the rotation while slightly leaning your inside knee and elbow into the direction of the turn. The subtle weight shift will keep you and your bike balanced and you'll sail through the turn. Being slightly off the seat will give you an extra measure of control.

Turn your body into a giant shock absorber. Loose arms and legs absorb the hits better, thereby decreasing the impact. Tightening up does not increase your control but rather detracts from it. Your body takes more of a beating than necessary, which tires you out faster.

Stay loose on rough downhills.

Along those same lines, make sure you keep your grip loose, too. Consciously work at it. There is nothing worse for your hands and wrists than the downhill death grip. Not only does this lead to severe and eventually chronic pain, tensing your hands gives your subconscious the go-ahead to tense everything else as well.

Remember, it takes a lot of energy to ride downhill. Keep as much in reserve as you can, particularly on long descents. Exhaustion is fear's greatest ally.

If there is a single word to bear in mind, it is "relax." Take deep breaths. Talk to yourself; tell yourself that you can do this and remind yourself that you are doing this for fun. We sometimes even sing to stay calm. After asking around, we discovered that almost everyone we know has a favorite downhill song.

Aside from serving as a minor distraction, singing or whistling requires you to breathe. You don't have to sing as long as you keep breathing, and remember that breathing out is just as important as breathing in. Our friend Julie is a perfect example — she is one of the best technical riders and certainly the fastest downhiller we know. Her secret? Julie doesn't sing, she uses the Làmaze breathing method whenever she starts to tense up.

As long as you stay relaxed, your mind and body are at their optimum flexibility. You can deal with anything that the trail throws at you. Letting go of your tension also releases your fear. Relaxing is also helpful in letting your instincts control your body's position. Your body is a slave to gravity and usually it will tell you where you need to be to remain stable.

Keeping Focused

> *"Look where you want to go, not where you want to miss."*
> Lisa Muhich, five-time national cyclocross champion

The principal name of the downhill game is focus - the ability to concentrate while keeping your mind and body relaxed. Focus is achieved by a simple three step process. The first point is to pay attention to the trail a comfortable distance <u>ahead</u> of you, generally ten to twenty feet. If you are watching the ground immediately in front of you, you get spooked by every little rock or twig which you

Pick a line to avoid obstructions.

should be just sailing right over. Focusing on the trail ahead, you give yourself that extra couple of seconds to plan your moves. Anticipation is a great confidence builder as it increases your comfort level.

The second step is to pick your line. This means that as you hurtle down the trail, you eyeball it, choosing the best way through it. Sometimes, like on a tight singletrack, the choices are slim and things may get a little bumpy, especially if the trail does double duty as an equestrian trail. Horses' hoofs can create some pretty nasty gouges and drop-offs. You might have no choice but to bounce your way over, into, and through them. But other times, particularly on fire roads, you have a wide area to deal with. You want to pick a line, or route, with the fewest obstructions on it.

For example, say you are descending on a fire road and see a rocky rut in the middle of it up ahead. You will want to choose a path that skirts the clearest side of the rut. Why go straight down the middle if you don't have to?

Picking your line works hand-in-hand with keeping your attention ahead of you as your line will be constantly changing and you need those extra couple of seconds to plan your strategy. The same is true for climbing, although not with the same urgency, as climbing is a slower process.

The third point of focus may be the most important: stay on target. Your bike will follow your eyes; wherever you're looking, more than likely that is where you will end up. Your subconscious plays follow-the-leader with your eyes. So when you see obstructions or obstacles, don't stare at them. Note them for safety's sake, then keep your eyes on the part of the trail that you want to take. This is not to say that you can never take your eyes off the ground, but if you are moving quickly, staying focused will ensure that you reach the bottom unscathed.

The Need For Speed

And since we have broached the subject, believe it or not, there really is a need for speed on downhills. Slower is rarely safer. We have noticed in our travels that a lot of people, both men and women although it seems more inherent to women, have a problem with maintaining enough downhill speed. We are not talking about setting new landspeed records, here. We are merely concerned about the difficulties one faces by concentrating too much on not picking up speed.

You see, going too slow is every bit as fraught with danger as going too fast, and certainly a lot trickier. Losing control of your mount is so much easier at ultra-slow speeds that there's even a branch of slow riding competition known as trials. The object in trials contests is to stay on the bike, without putting a foot down or falling over, going as slowly as possible over minor, and major, obstacles, obstacles not unlike those you might encounter on a trail.

There are few people involved in trials riding since not many people enjoy it due to the degree of difficulty. You have to be at the absolute peak of your performance as it demands the highest levels of balance, coordination, reflexes and concentration. That is what you are up against when you fight speed on a downhill.

When you are going too slow, it is also harder to maintain the proper position because gravity keeps pulling you forward. You let the trail take over, controlling your bike's actions, putting yourself at its mercy. Your center of gravity is too far forward, your balance is nil, and with all the weight moving towards the front, your back tire doesn't get the proper grip. Your bike is all over the trail in a side-to-side motion or worse, up and down. The tendency to over-compensate for all of this lost control further reduces your confidence as you overreact to every little bump and nudge until you finally come to a complete and shuddering stop or you fall over.

Keeping your speed too slow also does nothing but handicap your momentum. Momentum works hand-in-hand with traction to keep you moving and get you over the tricky spots with little or no difficulty. Riding your brakes, or worse, locking them up, stops traction and momentum dead in their tracks. You bounce off obstacles and ultimately the trail by robbing your tires of their grasp. When your tire hits a rock while moving at a snail's pace, the rock will kick your tire instead of the tire moving over the rock. Since you are already in overcompensation mode, you are likely as not to try to correct the wheel by oversteering just as sharply. Next thing you know, you are brushing yourself off.

Endos, those "over the handlebar falls," happen more often at slow speeds. As a matter of fact, all of the endos we have witnessed or heard about from the exploits of friends occurred the same way. The rider was moving along just fine or going a little on the slow side when a short drop-off appeared in the guise of a rock formation or drainage rut. The rider applied the brakes on the approach or, the ultimate in bad decisions, while going through it. Their front tire got

The power of momentum.

stuck, neglecting to spread the word to the back tire of the sudden change in plans. They ended up getting a close look at the ground.

So, when you forsake your momentum, you are fighting gravity. Believe us, gravity always wins. The way to confront a situation like this one is to pick up a little speed, not slow down. It's up to your back tire to see your front tire safely through which requires a head start; momentum.

Again, we're not talking about a daredevil descent. We just want you to bear in mind the rule of thumb governing tricky technical trails: pedal through. Whether it's a shallow water crossing, loose rocks, mud, or sand, pedalling through it sustains or increases your momentum to get you through safely. Mountain bike racer Jan Bolland passed along these helpful words of wisdom: "When I find myself in a sticky technical situation, I make a motorcycle noise and start pedalling."

To handle those nasty little drop-offs, maintain speed on the approach, level your pedals, lean back and coast right over.

Relax and enjoy the ride.

Building Confidence

The trick to enjoying downhill speed is one that tragically few of us master, and we are not just talking about mountain bike riding: believing in yourself. Interestingly enough, self-confidence is a learned behavior that you can and should practice.

Begin by thinking positively about your riding abilities. Just a few "I cans" a day will make a big difference, in how you feel and how you ride. If you make mistakes — and you will, you're only human — turn it around. Give it a positive spin and give yourself a break. You had trouble getting up off the seat during that last climb? At least you are still on the bike. Fell off the bike? It didn't kill you and, more than likely, didn't even hurt. Choked on that steep drop-off? You will work up to it, and gee, isn't it great to be out on such a beautiful day?

Slam the door on negative thoughts. Never say "I can't." Visualize yourself out there dropping the hammer with the best of them. Your brain believes whatever it's told; that's how we make it all happen. You just need to tell it the right things. Believe it or not, you can think yourself into a better, more graceful mountain biker. Elite athletes use visualization, why not give it a try as well?

The best way to conquer the fear of the big, bad downhill is to face it head on. Go downhill as often has you can, at every available opportunity. Start off gradually with short, easy descents. As your confidence and abilities increase, move on to some steeper stuff. Try to go a little faster every now and then.

If there is a spot in particular that gives you trouble, perhaps you walked your bike down it last time and now you have developed a case of the walking willies, take some time out to practice just that one piece of trail. It may take a few runs at it just to get the nerve up to do it the first time. That's okay. That's the way to learn downhilling.

When you've made it down once, go back over it a few more times, just to prove to your psyche that there's nothing to be afraid of, not for an incredibly awesome mountain biker like you.
Remember the mantra: relax. And enjoy the downhill ride. You've earned it.

"I finally concluded that all failure was from a wobbling will rather than a wobbling wheel."

Francis Willard
How I Learned To Ride The Bicycle

Chapter 6

Soft Landings

Just as in downhill skiing, learning how to fall is an important part of learning to ride a mountain bike. Spills, which might range from full-blown wipeouts to minor "oops" upsets, are a part of riding off-road. One of the benefits of riding on dirt, as opposed to pavement, is that if you do happen to fall, most of the time the only bruise you'll sustain is on your pride. Dirt is far more forgiving than pavement. Road cyclists get broken bones and road rash when they crash. We get muddy or dusty. Even rocky dirt is softer than asphalt. The abrasions suffered by mountain bikers are few, the broken bones even fewer.

But, just like any sport, there are exceptions. Some riders flirt with disaster due to their careless riding. Those who we know of who have experienced serious injuries weren't going to be satisfied until they had physical proof of their stupidity, riding recklessly without the slightest regard for their personal safety or the safety of others. They were an accident determined to happen. As far as the rest of us are concerned, a mountain biker's greatest worry is poison oak or poison ivy.

When you fall, roll with it.

Landing On Your Feet

We'll go over the "Oops, what happened there?" type of upset first. These pop up for any number of reasons, sometimes without warning, but they're usually recoverable. They just make you say, "Oops." Maybe a tire slipped or you grabbed too much brake at a bad moment. Whatever the cause, your safest recourse is to unclip or otherwise release at least one foot from the pedal at the slightest hint of trouble and simply put your foot down on the ground. And be aware of the nearest, softest landing, in the unlikely event things get out of hand.

Sometimes, like if you are dropping down a steep woods trail and start to lose control, you can just "bail out" by backing off the rear of the bike. You're already back there if you are descending properly so it's easy to slide off. Grab the bike by the seat post if you can, to keep it from rolling down and crashing.

There are other cases that sneak up on you but are still recoverable. In the event of an imminent endo (meaning you feel yourself about to come forward over the handlebar), you have three choices: attempt to recover control, try to land on your feet, or roll with it.

Some endos are recoverable simply by throwing your weight backwards at the first sign of lift-off, thus pushing the rear tire back onto the ground. Reflex plays a large part in this type of recovery; before you have a chance to think about it, you've done it.

In more extreme cases, you may have to "bail out" over the front. If you've passed the point of recovery and you find yourself mid-air with the back end of the bike nowhere near the ground and rising, let go of the handlebar and just step over it. Be ready to run when your feet touch the ground to soften the landing and to keep from getting tangled up with your bike.

Crashes

While you can recover from many potential falls, there will be times when you take a good spill. As you may have guessed, there is a technique to falling that minimizes the damage potential, both to you and your bike. Now, we'll go over the more serious "I missed the turn and I'm tumbling down the mountain" type of crash.

The key is to not panic and let your body get all tangled up with your bike. In just about every crash, you can see irretrievable trouble coming. A split-second of warning is all you need to part ways with your bike. By bailing out, you give yourself that much more control over your fall. You and your bike will both weather the storm in better condition without hitting each other.

A clean and easy escape should be the primary consideration if you, as we recommended in Chapter 2, use a form of binding on your pedals. You should release at least one foot prior to embarking on any section of trail where you feel your ability to remain upright might be tested. If you find yourself in trouble, getting the other foot out is easier than trying to release them both.

As you find yourself going into a fall and you know that you won't be able to land on your feet, the most important thing to do is to protect your head and neck. Cover your head with your hands and arms, tuck your legs up, and roll with the impact. This technique is called, "tuck and roll."

Try to stay as loose and relaxed as possible. We know that this sounds like we're asking a bit much when you find yourself careening off the trail, but it really is easier than it sounds. And the less you tense up, the less likely you are to be hurt. You'll probably do a somersault or two, you'll be shaken up, but, in most cases, you'll be fine. Duck your head, tuck in your legs, and roll.

Remember the phrase "duck, tuck, and roll" and repeat it to yourself. Picture yourself falling with proper technique, and bury it deep into the hidden recesses of your subconscious. No negative thoughts, remember? This way, when and if the time ever comes, you'll act properly without having to think about it.

We'll use our last endo scenario to illustrate this technique. Let's say that you are moving very quickly down a trail when you hit a ditch and your front tire stops abruptly. The suddenness of the action flips you, upside down, right over the front end of the bike. Relax as much as possible and try to roll with the force of contact, using the tuck and roll position. Believe it or not, such endos rarely do any damage beyond knocking the wind out of you and giving you a bit of a scare, provided, of course, that you wear your helmet at all times.

The survival instinct is our strongest and it will make us do whatever is necessary to keep us from harm, regardless of whether we're aware of it or not. If your body wants to suddenly change direction, jump back off your bike, let go, whatever, listen to your body. Don't second guess your instincts. As long as you don't fight it, you never force the situation to become a win or lose. It's just an "oops." Fight it and it may become a full-blown crash.

So, as we said at the start, we all take falls on mountain bikes so learning to fall properly is an important skill to master. The more you ride, the easier you'll handle both "oops" spills and more serious falls. As you build experience, trust your instincts. They won't let you down.

"Where else are women encouraged to be strong and independent — to sweat and spit and get dirty?"

Delaine Fragnoli
Associate Editor, *Mountain Biking*

Chapter 7

Bonking

Cars run out of gas. Runners hit the wall. Mountain bikers bonk. "Bonking" is a catchall word, encompassing everything from dizziness and headaches to dry heaves and heat stroke. It happens in any endurance sport when your energy has been drained. It happens to elite athletes and it can happen to you. When you feel disoriented, lethargic, and maybe just a little sick, you're bonking. You can bonk during a ride or shortly after one. If not handled properly at the outset, the feeling can last for a couple of days.

An ounce of prevention is, as Mr. Franklin so aptly put it, worth a pound of cure. But don't worry, we'll go over both.

The key to preventing a bonk is preparation. First and foremost, and we just can't stress this enough, bring plenty of water. You should never, ever, ever set out on any ride, even just down to the corner and back, without at least one full 20 ounce bottle of water.

Regardless of the time of year (you can actually dehydrate faster in the cold), if you're planning on riding for an hour or more, two standard-sized bottles are okay, two of the larger 27 ounce bottles are better, and two large 27 ounce bottles with a refill opportunity at a midway point is ideal.

Regardless of the time of year, carry a filled
water bottle (or as shown here, two.)

This may sound excessive to the uninitiated. However, the rule
of thumb is 16 ounces of fluid replacement for every half hour of
exercise. On top of that, you should start off a ride fully hydrated;
we each drink a full bottle of water or sport drink before we even
get our bikes out of the truck. Smart riders sip from their bike bottles
on the way to ride.

What about sports drinks and all the electrolytic replacement
drinks available? Packed with nutrients, and calories, these drinks
provide the "go power" for many mountain bike racers and are
becoming more and more popular with recreational riders. The

trick is to find one with a taste you like and which will agree with you. Try them around the house or on short local rides first. For us, water works best. And we like the price of it.

We've ridden with people who just simply, flat out, refuse to drink the water that we had to make them bring along. We don't understand this attitude at all. You can't tell us that just the thought of a dry and dusty twenty mile ride in 85-plus degree heat doesn't make your throat feel like the Mojave. We were on a ride with a friend of ours in just such conditions, with a few technical downhills and a couple of grueling uphills thrown in for good measure. We all knew that water was going to be available at a campsite that marked the halfway point. But we still could not convince our

You don't have to stop to rehydrate.

friend to even entertain the notion of drinking anything until he felt thirsty. He was saving his one 20 oz. bottle, he said, until he "really needed it." We offered him unlimited use of our own supplies, to no avail. Not surprisingly, and as we warned him, he bonked, thus illustrating the top reason for bonking: dehydration.

Unfortunately, most people are grossly misinformed about the nature of dehydration. Popular thought has it that you get thirsty, you perspire, then you dehydrate. Right elements, wrong sequence. Thirst is the last thing you feel before the heat stroke sets in. First, you perspire.

Perspiration is one of the body's systems of elimination of stored or built up toxins. Exercise accelerates your metabolism which, in turn, accelerates the elimination. You need to drink more water to make up for the water lost in the process.

We need water; without it, you can't even breathe. Water oxygenates the blood flowing into and out of your heart as it pumps merrily along. It's a necessary ingredient that the pancreas and liver use to purify the blood that your heart is so efficiently circulating. Water hydrates your organs and muscles, increasing the ease with which the blood pumps to them and through them, helping you to maintain your strength and stamina. Cramping and muscle strain are almost unheard of in a well-hydrated body. Get the point yet?

Mountain bike riding is a physically demanding sport. No matter how slow you go or how easy you take it, drink a lot and drink often. Your health and well-being depend on it.

As far as those concerns about needing to tinkle on the trail, always keep a tissue and a plastic bag handy in your bike bag. Be prepared, right? And between us girls, face uphill.

On longer or more strenuous rides, it's a good idea to bring along a sport drink, as well. Preferably one high in carbohydrates. Carbos equal instant energy. Which brings us to our next bonk prevention factor: food.

You shouldn't ride on a full stomach nor should you ride on an empty one. If we have to choose one or the other, though, we'd have to vote for full tummies. Not just as a safeguard against bonking, but also to maintain your cool. People who haven't eaten for a while tend to be a little hairtrigger. It's no fun to ride when you or someone you're riding with is crabby. With a full belly, you may feel a little languid out of the gate, but at least you're even-tempered. Ideally, however, you should not start a ride at either extreme. Eating within a half of an hour to an hour before a ride works out the best for us.

Now comes the all-important question of what to eat. As to riding specifically and life in general, "low fat" is the phrase that pays. Carbos and proteins are our friends. As stated earlier, carbohydrates are a quick and painless source of energy. And to dispel those myths and fears about carbos being high in calories, those calories are the energy source; they start burning as soon as they hit the digestive tract. They are so easy to digest, their benefits are immediate. A pre-ride potato is not unlike your morning coffee.

It's those fatty supplements, sauces, and garnishes that you need to replace or cast aside altogether. Fat counteracts the benefits of carbohydrates by creating difficulty in digestion. Fat stays with you, carbos don't.

Just as important, especially for those maintaining a low fat diet, are proteins. Proteins are stored energy, like having stamina in the bank. They too digest easily but more slowly, taking their place in line behind carbohydrates. Without the proper protein intake, you're more apt to be ready for a nap than a ride. Once you've spent the carbos, that's it. No more energy. Balancing the carbos with proteins will keep you riding in fine style.

So where do you find these great rewards?

The aforementioned potatoes, pasta, rice, and bagels are great sources of carbohydrates. Again, hold the butter, creamy sauces and sour cream.

You can't throw a rock without hitting protein. It can be found almost everywhere you look; in beans, whole grains, poultry, fish, nuts, and yogurt, just to name a few.

Fruits and vegetables are always a smart way to go, offering a veritable feast of proteins, carbos, vitamins, and minerals. The fruit supreme for a rider, or anyone else engaged in any form of exercise, is a banana. Aside from containing both protein and carbohydrates, bananas also have potassium, which revitalizes and heals tired muscles. But any fruit or vegetable will do. There's no such thing as a bad one.

If you just have to have a steak, save it for after the ride.

Besides fueling up before putting lycra to saddle, it's a wise idea to take something with you to snack on. Here is where compact, light fare like raisins, fig bars, nuts, or energy bars really come in handy. A little power boost by way of a stop-and-smell-the-flowers nibble is amazingly refreshing, even if you didn't realize you needed it.

A chat 'n chew stop.

Be smart and keep it simple. A cross-country ride is not the time for a salami sandwich.

Energy bars seem to be the snack of choice among racers and recreational riders alike. You can find a variety of them available at bike shops and health food stores. Some convenience stores have hopped on the fitness bandwagon by carrying a couple of the more popular brands and flavors.

So now you know how to prevent a bonk, but what do you do if you or someone you love does bonk? That depends on where you are when bonk time rolls around.

If you're out on the trail and you start to feel lightheaded, suddenly fatigued, or nauseous, stop immediately. Pull over into the nearest shade and sit a spell. Chances are, you're feeling a little too warm. Bend over and squirt some water onto the back of your neck. The neck is your body's personal thermostat; to turn it down you need to cool it off. That's why you'll sometimes see people with wet bandannas tied around their necks. It's not just a look.

Even though you probably won't have any around you, we feel we should say this anyway: under no circumstances should you ever hold ice on the back of your neck. Putting such intense cold against a hot neck can trigger shock. The object here is to cool down, not pass out.

If you brought along a sport beverage, now would be a good time to drink it. Wash it down with water or drink water only. Drink slowly, do not gulp unless you want to see it again. But don't be stingy. If you have any food, start chowing down. Take your time. Take deep breaths. Relax.

When the worst of the feeling passes and you feel almost human again, head on home. Trying to finish out the ride is begging for trouble.

In the comfort and safety of your own home, kick back, drink lots of fluids, and indulge in some carbo-loading. Get some rest and you're good as new.

If you bonk after the ride and you're all ready at home, which has been known to happen, you're ahead of the game. Follow the same procedure; fluids, food, and rest. Then you can tell all your friends about your epic ride that was so extreme, it made you sick. They'll shake their heads, call you crazy, and ask if they can go with you next time.

"When I think about mountain biking, the first thing that comes to mind are the weekend rides that I do in the winter with my friends. We always meet at a coffee shop for some pre-ride nutrients. Then we spend 3 to 5 hours biking and hiking on our favorite single track in the North Vancouver Rain Forest. Every ride is an adventure. After the ride, we always seem to find our way to another coffee shop. We sit down to refuel with big grins on our faces and add to our ever-growing repertoires."

Alison Sydor
1994 Cross-Country World Champion
Team Volvo-Cannondale

Chapter 8

Finding Trails

All of this fabulous information doesn't amount to a hill of chain links if you don't have a favorite place to ride or if, try as you might, you just can't get at least one friend or loved one to share in your new avocation. The two most common complaints from would-be mountain bikers are "I don't know where to ride" and "I don't have anyone to ride with." The two are related. Having a riding companion quite often opens the door to riding locations; there's a 50/50 chance that one of the two of you will have an idea about where to go. And if neither of you do, it's a discovery process that you go through together.

Bike buddies are also helpful in learning new or different handling techniques. Not only are you more experimental when bolstered by a buddy, sometimes you get a good lesson in what not to do or realize you've been doing something wrong when you see someone else make the same mistake. There are, of course, countless benefits from riding with a more experienced pal who's not uncomfortable in the role of coach.

But where do you find these pearls of the pedal?

A bike buddy can help you find new trails to try.

Bike Clubs

One easy solution to both problems is to check out your local bike clubs. Most bike clubs offer a regular schedule of rides and related activities which may include meetings, social events, fundraisers, races, and we hope, trail and land access support.

Club memberships are based on a variety of themes or ideologies. They range from the general enthusiasts to highly specialized interests based on geographic area, marital status, gender, political leanings, bike brand, favorite color; you name it, there's probably a club for it.

Of particular interest to women is the Women's Mountain Biking and Tea Society (WOMBATS), one of the largest bike clubs in the world with over 1000 members internationally. Founded by pro racer and NORBA pioneer Jacquie Phelan, WOMBATS was formed as a venue to demystify the sport and support the interests and enthusiasm of women mountain bikers. WOMBATS' focus is on beginning riders and the recreationally-minded; riders are encouraged to participate in skills clinics and group rides. The club also serves as a women's riding network — whether you're across the country or across the Atlantic, a fellow female riding buddy is just a phone call away. The WOMBATS mailing address and "Batline" phone numbers are listed in the Resource section.

There are several resources to consult in your search for the club that best fits your style. Once again, the yellow brick road begins at your bike shop. If someone there doesn't know of any clubs, which is unlikely, many groups are listed in bike-related books, magazines, and periodicals.

But wait, you say you're not the club type? Not sure you want to commit yourself to being that social on a regular, maybe long-term, basis? Have no fear, there are other avenues to explore.

Tour Groups

Mountain bike tour groups are a great introduction to trail areas and other riders who, like you, are new to the sport, new to the area, or are on vacation. This is ideal for beginners as rides are led by at least one experienced biker.

There's a smorgasbord of tours and packages available, based on desired length and distance, degree of difficulty, and whether you're looking for a ride or an adventure. Outings can last anywhere from a couple of hours to several days.

Tour companies rent bikes, if you don't want to take your own or you're on vacation yourself and left your bike at home. They'll also equip you with the necessary food and water and offer sag wagon support. (A sag wagon is a truck or a van that carries extra food and first aid supplies, offers technical and medical support, and transports people and bikes between points on a one-way ride.

On longer rides, the sag wagon carries everybody's overnight gear and anything else you might require.)

Usually, tour groups throw in a water bottle as a keepsake. You know you're a real mountain biker when you've built up a collection of water bottles from all over. The more banged up they get, the better the stories that go with them.

Tour groups will most often take you into the heart of prime mountain biking areas. One good trail usually leads to another. And, if nothing else, you'll learn about at least one trail that you can come back to on your own.

Again, ask around at your bike shop or flip through the yellow pages for bike tour companies near you or in the places that you're interested in riding. In the Resource section, we have compiled a list, with addresses and phone numbers, of some of the larger or better-known touring companies.

Tour companies can introduce you to scenic trail and back road riding.

Bike shops are good sources of "where to ride" information.

Bike Shops

Bike shops themselves sometimes coordinate regular or semi-regular ride groups. It might be a formal effort under the shop's banner, requiring a sign-up, or an informal group of folks who get together to ride once a week. The "weekly ride," as they're often dubbed, is a great way to explore new trails, not to mention meet other mountain bikers.

When inquiring about weekly rides, be sure to get the lowdown as to any skill-level requirements. Ride locations are usually chosen on a group consensus and the group may consist of riders who love white-knuckle downhills. That's the kind of thing you'd like to know about riding companions before setting out.

Bike shops are also the first stop on the grapevine for local race promoters. If there's a race or race series upcoming, your bike shop will know when and where. Even if you don't have aspirations of one day going for the gold yourself, attending a mountain bike race is like attending a mountain bike fair; racers and spectators alike compare notes on equipment, technique, and rides. Local races take place on local trails. And in the cases of trails being specially made for a race, the trail often remains after the race is over.

Cross country ski trails are often great places to ride.

Guidebooks

If you prefer to find a place to dig your tires into on your own, there are dozens of excellent guidebooks and trail maps available at book stores and bike shops. Alas, not all of them are clear, coherent, or accurate when it comes to trail markings or distances. Time and trail users can change the appearance of an ambiguous trail head and you should anticipate that the distance to or from markers is approximate; we've followed more than one guidebook's directions that were up to a mile off from the printed description. Be patient and flexible when following a map or a book. This is a somewhat new sport, after all. And, although it doesn't seem like it should be, distance is sometimes relative to the individual. At any rate, guidebooks and maps can give you a good general feel for the trail area that you're investigating and you can come across some really sweet rides this way.

Back road exploring by mountain bike.

Another good bet is an organization called the Rails-To-Trails Conservancy. Rails-To-Trails is a non-profit group whose mission in life is converting abandoned railroad corridors into multi-use trails, working hand-in-hand with land access groups, public agencies, and railroad companies. For those who have seen some of the old railways around the Sierras in Northern California, you know that those corridors can be in some pretty spectacular places.

You can write to Rails-To-Trails at the address listed in the back of this book for information on converted trails. They'll send you a catalogue, listing guides to the converted trail areas across the country. Or you can purchase a book that describes them all.

Mountain Bike Vacations

Why not consider a bike vacation? What could be better than exploring exotic locations, from deserts to islands, on your bike? The ads lure you: "First trip of its kind" (France); "Ride where only burros have gone" (Venezuela); or "Cycle Off-Road Australia." Mountain biking fever has spread across the globe. If you've got the time, the money, and the inclination, the whole world is out there, waiting to be explored by knobby tires.

Again, tour companies are usually the way to go for hassle-free vacations. You can purchase packages ranging from budget camping in national parks to luxury five-star resorts with their own singletrack. In most cases, accommodations, meals and technical support are included in the package but ask ahead to be certain. They can help you find a vacation spot or adventure that's right for you. Once more, refer to the list in the Resource section.

For those with weekend getaways in mind, more and more ski resorts, realizing that they possess an off-season gold mine, now cater to mountain bikers in those long, dry months between winters. The off-season, or bike season, depending on your point of view, starts around Memorial Day, in most places, and continues through mid-October or so.

If you have visions of bikes screaming down a vertical mountain face, relax — most resorts don't allow mountain bikers onto the downhill ski courses. Instead, more and more resorts have developed miles of trail networks cleared specifically for us consisting of sweeping switchbacks, single and doubletrack, fast fire roads, and meandering ridge trails. You have a choice of either winding your way up and down or taking the ride up in a chairlift.

Billing themselves as mountain bike parks for the summer season, ski resorts make a variety of services available, tailored to meet our needs. Chairlifts are retrofitted to accommodate bikes (riders go up first, followed by their bikes on a separate chair), there are full-service bike shops on the premises, and often both a snack bar (with sandwiches and high carbo snacks to take with you) and a restaurant.

Ski resorts usually have a rental package consisting of nicely-outfitted bikes, helmets, an all-day lift ticket, and a keepsake water bottle. The deal often has a free lesson on basic bike handling as well. Expect to find riding clinics and guided rides available. It's a great way to break into mountain biking or polish up some skill, all in a beautiful vacation environment.

If you don't live near any ski resorts, a travel agent can help you find a place to ride. Each season, more and more open for mountain biking. If you time it right, you might even be able to catch a leg of the National Off Road Bicycle Association (NORBA) Nationals or the Grundig World Cup Series races. Ski resorts across the country play host to local, national and international races throughout the season.

As you've probably surmised, a bountiful source of trail information comes from other riders. Whether you're hobnobbing around the shop, out on a trail, or getting a refill in the break room at work, once you get a mountain biker talking, they can't help but tell you all about a gnarly ride they just did or their favorite trail of all time. It's an irresistible urge we all have that can start as innocently as "How was your weekend?"

"Mountain biking has allowed me to see some of the most beautiful places in the world, and meet some of the nicest people..."

Susan DeMattei
Top ranking professional cross country racer
Diamond Back Racing

Chapter 9

Mountain Bike Manners

We've explained what to ride, how to ride, and where to ride. Now here are some guidelines to ensure an enjoyable trail time is had by all.

Canine Encounters

We are fortunate, as mountain bikers, to not have as many run-ins with man's best friend as our pavement pounding counterparts. We are unfortunate in that the type of dogs we do encounter are a bit more aggressive than their citified cousins. If you want an adrenaline rush, pedal around a bend on a dirt road and see a couple of farm dogs lying in the road, their road, just waiting for you. Leash laws don't apply where we ride.

The least threatening situation is a dog whose owner is, if not attached at the other end of a leash, at least fairly close by. Pet owners are generally not looking for any trouble in our litigation-happy society. If the animal is at all ornery or unpredictable, their master will usually restrain or subdue them for you when they see you coming. You need only to slow down, so as not to arouse Spot's chasing instincts, and ease past.

If you are the type who is afraid of dogs or you just do not like them, put on your best "I love all creatures, great and small" act. It is for the dog's benefit, not the owner's. Human technology pales when compared to a dog's radar.

The other type of situation, decidedly less pleasant, is when one or (gulp) more dogs are roaming unattended, the sunlight glinting off their large, drooling teeth as they bark their heads off at you. It is imperative that you at least appear to be unimpressed by the pack. As mentioned before, animals are pretty easy to trick but you have make a little effort to be convincing. Especially if you are dealing with more than one.

Calmly but quickly dismount, placing the bike between you and them. Attempt to move away slowly, keeping a watchful eye. Do not turn your back on Barky and his pals. Dogs love to exploit even the most minute weakness in your defenses. Sometimes they will let you go without too much fuss, just a lot of noise. Then they will cease barking once you are off their turf.

If they have got their panting little hearts set on your lycra for lunch, you can give Cathy's trick a try. Riding a motorcycle in the California Sierra foothills, she learned that a water gun was all she needed to deter the local canines from literally nipping at her heels. Carrying that principle over to mountain bikes, give them a blast in the face from your water bottle. They will be startled into silence and, in our experience, they skulk away unhurt but humbled.

We are not guaranteeing that this will work one hundred percent of the time, but so far, it has worked for us. Besides, as dog owners ourselves, we cannot condone nor do we recommend any sort of physical provocation or confrontation. Most of the time, that will just make a touchy situation all the way bad.

Dogs aside, encountering wildlife is one of the draws of mountain biking. There is something mystical about cruising along your favorite trail and having a deer leap across your path. Bikes being quieter than feet or hoofs, we have accidentally snuck up on coyotes spying their prey. Fortunately, we were spared the lesson in the food chain without disrupting it. Everyone went back to what they were doing when they saw that we were not staying.

Encountering wildlife is one of the draws of mountain biking.

Mountain Bike Etiquette

Once you have had a taste of the grandeur of the wilderness, testament to the sheer majesty and glory of Mother Nature, you can begin to appreciate the mountain biker's golden rule: stay on designated trails only!

Multi-use trail placement is generally well thought out before being constructed. Trails are placed in such a way that the users can achieve that feeling of getting away from it all while creating the least amount of environmental impact, preserving the quality of life for the animals, plants, and insects that inhabit the area. In most cases, access is carefully weighed against the balance of nature. Every time someone goes off the marked trails, whether on feet, hoofs, or tires, they upset the integrity of that balance. It may not mean that much to you, but to the flora and fauna into whose refuge you are barging, it could mean life or death.

Whether you care or not, trails are marked for a reason. Violation of those markings has dire consequences for your fellow mountain bikers, as well. Ironically, with the sudden surge of the sport's popularity has come the problem of trail closures. The abuses of a few are infringing on the rights of the many. Every time someone goes off a trail or onto a trail expressly forbidden to bikes, it strengthens the arguments against mountain bike access.

Stay off trails closed to mountain bikes.

We know it is sometimes tempting: you are positive that no one will see you, and you think to yourself, "Just this once." Just that once may be the reason that bikes are banned from the park. Because you did not see anyone did not mean that no one was there. You would be surprised at how many people know where you are and are not allowed. And if one of those people is a ranger, you get the added bonus of a rather hefty fine.

A graphic example of this disturbing trend is Mount Tamalpais in Marin County, California, the motherland of mountain biking. Due to the public's perception of mountain bikers' trail abuses and excessive speeds, the hikers and area residents are succeeding in closing more and more trails to bikes and are working toward closing the gates to us entirely. Similar stories are being told from around North America and Europe.

A good sign for mountain biking.

Fortunately, there is something everybody can do and as a mountain biker, you are honor bound to support your local and federal land access efforts. On the local level, you can join volunteer trail restoration parties or organize one yourself. This usually involves a one day effort, every few months or so, and can be coordinated with park rangers or your Parks and Recreation Services office. They can tell you how to restore trails that have been damaged by use or the elements, help get you started and, quite often, provide you with the necessary tools.

Federally, time and money are precious to the ongoing lobbying efforts to overturn trail closures and to open new trails. For more information and details, contact the International Mountain Biking Association (IMBA) or the Bureau of Land Management (BLM). Their addresses can be found at the end of this book. Both agencies can answer questions regarding land access issues in your area. IMBA has a network of bike club affiliates across the country who can help get you involved in local trail maintenance programs. Headway is being made but we have got a long way to go; trails worth riding are worth the fight.

Another part of your job as a responsible off-road rider is to promote a positive image. Leaving people with a good impression has an effect on all mountain bikers. The public's perception of us has everything to do with trail access. Some people do not need a heck of a lot of pushing to prove their prejudices. Do not justify those prejudices; turn them around. Do your bit to show them that one bad biker does not represent the sport.

When encountering others, be they hikers, equestrians or fellow bikers, smile and say hello. If you are approaching someone from behind, give them some notice of your approach. A chipper "Excuse me" is more polite and gets a friendlier response that the roadie bark "on your left." This call is often, and in our opinion, rightfully, construed as rude; the road call was designed for the cutthroat atmosphere of road racing where there are packs of riders all vying for position. Some people have opted for a bell, which is also handy when you are coming down a blind switchback at a fairly good clip to warn anyone who may be around the bend.

When coming across horses, slow way down or stop and ask the rider's permission to pass. Under no circumstances should you ever attempt to pass a horse unless you've been invited, at which time you should give the horse a wide berth and pass slowly or walk. It's not a question of manners but of safety. While your steed is totally under your control, a horse is a living creature. There is no telling what may spook one. A friend of ours has a horse that freaks out when it sees purple flowers.

We think that IMBA's Rules of the Trail says it best:
1. RIDE ON OPEN TRAILS ONLY
2. LEAVE NO TRACE
3. CONTROL YOUR BICYCLE
4. NEVER SPOOK ANIMALS
5. PLAN AHEAD
6. SHOW COURTESY AND RESPECT
   TO ALL TRAIL USERS, AT ALL TIMES.

Mountain Biking Ambassadors

It only takes a moment to make a lasting impression and prime opportunities for a little extra mountain biking public relations do pop up. We experienced just such an occasion not long ago.

There is a coastal mountain range in our home town which can be accessed by a shortcut down a rural road that leads to a commercial ranch, the last twenty feet of which are considered ranch property. The property owner had chained off the last part of the road to discourage undue bike and foot traffic heading to the mountain.

One summer evening, we were on the return descent on the switchback trail when we rounded a turn and discovered the path was blocked by three recently shorn sheep. It did not take a rocket scientist to figure out that these were escapees from the ranch. We were in a quandary as to how to get around each other when we heard a voice yelling, "Do you see some sheep up there?"

Looking down over the edge of the trail to the lower part of the fire road, we spotted the shepherd, a harried-looking woman clearly exasperated with her charges.

Cathy responded, "They're right here."

Robin piped in, "Do you want us to bring them down?" How hard could it be, right?

The shepherd was surprised and relieved at the offer. "Could you, please?"

We said a jaunty, "We'll be right there," and mounted our scoots. We had recently seen the movie City Slickers which, of course, made us experts in riding a herd, or mini-herd, as the case may be.

Robin "heeyah"-ed herself hoarse while Cathy whistled and whooped, and we successfully drove the sheep back to their owner. The sheep were highly agitated, not your average docile breed. Chatting with the woman from the ranch, we found out that these sheep had been impounded from a farm further north where they had been neglected and abused. As she was telling us about how unpredictable they could be, they tried to get away again. The woman caught one while the other two went charging back up the mountain along the fire road.

We jumped back on our bikes and gave chase, inadvertently pushing them up. Knowing the trails better than the cloven-hooved out-of-towners, Cathy was able to get right behind them while Robin took a higher trail that dropped her down right in front of them when they reached the top. We managed to stop them in their tracks and turn them around. We then started the downhill drive once again.

Now accustomed to their slippery ways, Cathy rode alongside them, cutting off their hopes of escaping up the face of the mountain, thick with foliage and underbrush. We were not worried about them attempting to jump down the slope as domestic live-stock are not exactly known for their down-gradient prowess.

On our way, we encountered another mountain biker, visibly impressed, who delivered a message from the shepherd woman: not to worry about it if we could not catch them. It was starting to get dark and she was more worried about us than the sheep.

We scoffed at this and continued our drive. When we had the woman once again in view and shouting distance, we informed her of our success and started to relax. The sheep sensed this and took advantage of it, turning sharply, and darned quickly, straight up through the high brush and trees.

Cathy valiantly tried to follow them on foot, but they easily outran her, turning in two different directions at once. They were out of sight in seconds.

We dejectedly plodded back to the ranch woman, victory having slipped through our fingers. She thanked us profusely for our efforts and told us not to worry about the sheep; she would fetch them the next morning. As it turned out, we later heard, it actually took her three days to catch the little rogues.

Here is the happy ending. The next time we took the shortcut to the mountain, the chain was down from the private road and down it has stayed. We also heard a story about these two women on mountain bikes who helped a woman from the ranch catch her sheep.

"Mountain biking is a very egalitarian sport that brings women into the realm of realizing what's possible, what we're capable of — whether riding to the grocery store or racing down mountains at breakneck speeds."

Jennifer Prosser
Team Manager
Team Volvo/Cannondale

Chapter 10

A Day At The Races

Racing isn't for everybody. But attending a race is. As we touched on in Chapter 8, a mountain bike race, particularly one sanctioned by NORBA, is made up of equal parts competition and bike fair. You'll be able to observe a variety of bikes and accessories in action; you'll see some things you've only heard about and some things you've never even thought of. And the sponsors and the racers themselves are more than willing to share their thoughts on their equipment or technique.

From spring to fall, there are dozens of mountain bike races every month in each region of the country. If your hometown is a stop on either the NORBA National Championship Series or the international World Cup Series (the locations change every year), you'll not only be treated to world class competition and courses (should you choose to compete), but also riding exhibitions, riding and maintenance clinics, and information and exhibit booths set up by sponsors, land access groups, and race organizers. Several of the larger sponsors travel with prototypes of new bikes or accessories, previewing them or getting in a little race-testing before the big fall Interbike trade show.

On race day, the whole family can get involved; one of the largest component manufacturers sponsors a Youth Series for kids under the age of 12. After Mom, Dad, or both get through riding their own race (or watching them), they can cheer on their progeny. The Youth Series is strictly for fun, meant as a way to introduce everyone to the joys of mountain biking and mountain bike racing.

You can find the latest in bikes and accessories at mountain bike races.

For those interested in competing, the world of mountain bike racing is renowned for its congeniality. Racers engaged in combat encourage each other, and, while technical assistance is strictly verboten, advice and moral support flow freely. More experienced racers can be downright solicitous over beginners, and women in particular are welcomed with enthusiasm.

Mountain bike racing has been a male-dominated sport with a large number of male participants and a small field of women racers. Women's participation is growing but still is far behind: at most races, the men's fields are well over twice the size of the women's fields. Sponsors often decided that cash prizes will be based on field size and so there is often a large disparity in award amount between men and women. After a constant struggle, this is starting to change at the professional level where prizes are getting closer to being equal.

What is obvious is that there is a real opportunity for any woman who wants to jump into the sport of mountain bike racing. There's also a lot of interest in attracting more women riders. Race clinics and workshops across the country are aimed at building riding and racing skills, and as we write this book, "Women-Only" mountain bike races are starting to emerge. Have you thought about donning a number and competing?

Getting Started

As we said, racing isn't for everybody. But if you have toyed with the idea, don't be scared off thinking that you can't do it because you don't have that killer instinct. And certainly don't think that you shouldn't enter a race because you don't think you'd win. Not too many people win the first race they enter. Or the second or third.

Racing is a growth process; it's about your individual perform-ance. Someone who races "against" others is setting themselves up for a lot of disappointment — there will always be somebody better. But someone who approaches a race as an achievement in personal performance...well, that person is going to have a lot more fun. And that's the primary reason you should be there on the starting line.

We're not saying that you shouldn't want to win but the old saying is still true, winning isn't everything. The vast majority of competitors aren't racing to win, they just want to finish. This should be the first goal of anyone starting out. There are other important considerations, especially for beginning racers. Did you overcome a fear or cruise through an obstacle that you didn't think you could? Did you learn a new handling tip or try something new? Did you have a good time?

Getting started in racing is a snap. The first step, of course, is to go to the bike shop. If they don't know of any upcoming races, chances are they'll at least have NORBA racing license applications handy. A license is required to enter any race affiliated with NORBA, whether it's a race day only license or one that you carry with a membership.

An annual membership costs $29 and with the license, you also get a subscription to *NORBA News*, United Airlines discounts for travel to and from NORBA events nationwide, the *Off-Road Competition Guide*, accident insurance at NORBA events, the all-important NORBA decal, and the eligibility to qualify for National and World Championships and NORBA State Series. Listed in every monthly issue of the *NORBA News* is a nationwide schedule of races, including their location and a phone number for more information.

Racers are categorized by age (Junior, 12-18; Senior, 19-34; Veteran, 35-44; Master, 45 and up) and by level of expertise (Beginner, Sport, Expert, and Pro/Elite). The Beginner class is open to all entry level racers to get their feet wet and hone their skills. After placing in the top five in five races, you have to move up to Sport. The Sport class is made up of faster, intermediate riders. Sport racers have to advance to Expert after three top-three finishes or six top-six finishes. The Expert group consists of the advanced, highly skilled racers. Experts placing in the top five in three National Championship Series races will be bumped up to Pro/Elite, the crème de la crème of mountain bike racers. Others wishing to enter in the Pro/Elite class must submit a racing rèsumè. To avoid unfair advantages, the racing rules stipulate that those racers who do not advance as required face suspension.

While there are several types of competition, the most widely held race events are the Cross Country, Downhill, and Dual Slalom.

Cross country races, which attract the most participants, are staged on circuit courses, the number of laps required corresponding to your gender and class; men do more laps than women, Sports

Cross country races are staged on circuit courses.

do more laps than Beginners, and so on. The track is comprised of fire roads, singletrack, and technical sections with enough climbing and descending to keep things interesting. One lap is generally ten miles, give or take a few. Most beginners wanting to get a taste of the racing experience will start with cross country.

Downhill races are the most popular spectator events due to the speed and ease of viewing the action. The courses are fairly short, under five miles, and consist of wide, fast fire roads or ski trails with long momentum-building straightaways followed by turns to make it even more challenging. Occasionally, a course designer will throw in a little singletrack near the bottom to test the riders' bike-handling skills at race speeds. Downhill racers can exceed 50 miles per hour on a fire road course; while great for spectators, this is not an event for the faint-hearted.

The dual slalom race is a lot like a skiing dual slalom; two riders weave their way around flags snaking along a downhill course, side by side. Where cross country is largely decided by stamina and the downhill is decided by nerve, the dual slalom is a test of bike handling skills. The courses are loose and fast and the winner is often the person who managed to stay on their bike.

It's important to note that you can participate in different classes for different events. In other words, you might be a Sport in cross country racing and a Beginner in downhill.

In keeping with the spirit of the backcountry enthusiast, one of the most important rules is that of self-sufficiency. It's taken quite seriously and it's stringently enforced. Any emergency trailside repairs must be done individually, without any outside assistance. And if you didn't bring the right tool, you're not allowed to borrow it from another racer. You are also not allowed to "cannibalize" another bike, i.e. swap parts. You have to finish the race on the same bike with the same parts that you started with, even if it means carrying the bike across the finish line.

To enter a race, you can register either by mail ("pre-registration") or at the appropriately marked area on the day of the race. Unfortunately, racing isn't free but most of the time, pre-registration is cheaper. Entry fees vary from race to race. You can also get a one-time NORBA racing license if you are just trying things out.

Another reason to pre-register for races is that there might be a limit to the number of participants allowed. Fortunately or unfortunately, depending on your point of view, women don't have to worry about this as much as men do. But remember, we want to fill up the field. It will be a milestone for women's mountain biking when a woman walks up to the registration table for a local race and she's told, "Sorry, your class is full."

Whether you're a first-time Beginner or a seasoned Pro, plan on pre-riding the course. If at all possible, arrive at the race site at least a day or two early. Practicing the course is valuable for any number of reasons. You'll move faster with more confidence on a trail that you're more familiar with. You can go over it slowly a time or two, picking and choosing your lines. You can practice pace and endurance strategies. If you can't pre-ride until race day, warm up but don't wear yourself out.

If your chosen race is the cross country, make sure you'll have plenty of water. On longer race courses, there's usually a designated water and food hand-off spot. Station relatives or friends there with a full bottle and a banana and tell them to cheer really loud when you go whizzing past.

"One half of the world cannot understand the pleasures of the other."

Jane Austen
Emma [1815]

Chapter 11

Upgrades

No, this isn't more about climbing. In this chapter, we'll explore the truths and myths about enhancing your riding comfort and prowess through the judicious use of accessory items. We say judicious because, let's face it, you can replace virtually every part on your bike with something made of lighter, possibly more durable (and definitely more expensive) material. Your bike is probably quite able-bodied in its stock, or "production," condition, but certain upgrades can make it better. We have focused on five items: bar ends, brake levers, tires, saddles, and suspension forks, any one of which can help make you a better mountain bike rider.

Bar Ends

If you encounter a fair amount of climbing on your favorite trails, the first item you should run right out and get, if they didn't come with your bike, are bar ends. Bar ends are pretty much what they sound like. They are extensions that clamp or otherwise attach perpendicularly to the ends of your handlebar to accentuate balance and leverage by encouraging you to bring your weight forward when climbing.

Bar ends come in a variety of shapes and sizes.
Shown here are a curved pair.

Bar ends come in a variety of shapes and sizes, colors and price ranges. When you're looking at them, don't be shy. You have to handle them before you buy them to make an educated purchase. The goal is to find the bar ends that best fit your hands. Some people might want bar ends with an L-shaped bend, which offers more hand position choices. Others might want a smaller type with a subtle curve, known as a "ski bend." Still others may like the style that points straight out. It all depends on how they feel to you. Will they be comfortable on an out-of-the-saddle climb with your weight bearing down on them?

Once you've found the perfect bar ends, comes the time when you have to put them on. Bar end installation is simple, so easy that very few of them come with instructions. You need only to tighten one bolt. The trick is that you have to know how to move your grips over to allow the bar ends room on your handlebar.

Never, ever cut your grips. Short grips, besides being uncomfortable, crowd your hands and limit your movements. In other words, they're useless. The only people who cut grips are those who aren't in on the two secrets.

Secret #1: removing the closed end of the grip. Gently tap the end of the handlebar with a hammer a few times. The combination of the metal hammer hitting the metal handlebar does the work for you. It cleanly cuts the rubber core from the inside until it pops right out. This allows you to pass the handlebar through the grip freely.

Secret #2: hairspray off, gel on. This is, by far, the most entertaining of all "mechanical" tips. Carefully ease a medium-sized flat-head screwdriver inside the grip and lift the rubber up enough to be able to shoot a spritz of hairspray into it. You don't need to lift it up very high, a little bit is all you need. Use a pump spray, as opposed to an aerosol; pumps are more accurate and easier to control.

Remove the screwdriver after spritzing and start twisting the grip back and forth. It won't move very much at first but as the hairspray gets distributed, the grip will suddenly move around like it's been greased. Slide the grip on over, exposing enough room on the outside end of the bar for the bar end to clamp on, usually about an inch. The outer side of the bar end clamp should be flush with the end of the handlebar.

Most bar ends come with two rubber or plastic plugs. These are to plug the holes in the ends of the handlebar and to cover the sharp edges of the bar end clamp, keeping sensitive body parts safe from harm in the event of contact. Always use these plugs. If they fall out, replace them immediately.

To ensure that the grips will stay put in their new homes, once again gently lift up the grip with the screwdriver. This time, put a little hair gel on the inside surface of the grip with your finger. Just a dab will do ya. Twist the grip around to evenly distribute the gel. When it dries, your grips will be firmly bonded to the bar. Hair spray will break that seal if you need to move them again.

Pretty neat, huh? It may take a few rides to set completely, so if they move around at first, don't get spooked.

A curved bar end mounted next to a two-fingered brake lever.

Sometimes, (as shown in the photo above) you may need to move the brake and shift levers over a bit toward the center to accommodate the new placement of the grips. The bolt for each lever (or the single bolt on integrated units) is underneath the bar. Simply loosen the bolts, slide the units over, leaving about a quarter-inch or more clearance between shifters and brakes, and then retighten the bolts. Tighten them as hard as you can. It can get annoying when your levers get loose on a ride, especially if you didn't take our advice in Chapter 2 and don't have a wrench handy.

Straddle the bike when you're retightening the bolts so you can reset the levers at a comfortable angle. Make sure that your brake levers aren't forcing your hands into a backwards bend. When your hands are on the brakes, the line running from your hands to your elbows should be smooth and straight.

When setting the angle of the bar ends, play around with them; find an angle that works best for you. Start off at a 45 degree angle which is half the distance between straight up and pointing straight out ahead. Sit on the bike and see how it feels. From that point, move the bar ends down, closer to pointing straight ahead, as much as is comfortable. This makes your climbing position more aggressive by bringing your weight further forward.

Do not raise the angle any higher than 45 degrees, which is kind of pushing it, anyway. The further back the angle, the further back it's going to push you which only hurts your climbing balance and therefore nullifies the benefit of having bar ends. Most riders find that a 30 degree angle works best.

If you've never considered bar ends, we strongly suggest you do. We're big fans of them. Not only do they feel good and work well, they look cool, too.

Brake Levers

The next upgrade items you should consider are two-fingered brake levers. Again, these come as stock items on a lot of bikes and are exactly what they sound like. They are shorter brake levers with the bend placed such that your index and middle fingers fit quite nicely, snug as a bug, which lets the rest of your hands stay on the handlebar. These are not only a major convenience control-wise, they are essential for those of us with smaller hands.

The choices that are available are not quite as varied as with bar ends, and your color choices are pretty much limited to black or chrome finishes.

Brake levers are a tad bit more difficult to install so you may want to choose to have them professionally changed. But don't be intimidated if you are interested in doing it yourself. Robin changed the brake levers on both of our bikes (over Cathy's objections), knowing basically nothing about them. By the second bike, she was an expert. Just take it slow and easy, doing one at a time so you can use the other one as a reference. Most of all, enjoy the intimacy level with your bike.

Since there are different set ups with varying degrees of complexities out there, we won't go into installation here. We will recommend, though, that you pick up a good, well-illustrated, and easy-to-understand maintenance manual. The good ones will tell you what you'll need before you start so you won't find yourself halfway through realizing you don't have the right tool to continue. We've found Rodale Press' *Complete Guide To Bicycle Maintenance And Repair* fits the bill nicely.

Even if you're not planning on doing a bottom bracket overhaul next week, it's nice to have a manual around to get better acquainted with the nuts and bolts of your bike. Whether you use it or not, knowledge is still power.

Tires

Our next area of upgrade scrutiny is an important one: your tires. If you plan to spend much time in the dirt, proper tires are a basic necessity. You may think that all tires are, more or less, the same but this just isn't the case. There are a bunch of different tread patterns and widths running loose in the world, each serving a different purpose.

There are soft-condition tires, hard-condition tires, mud tires, and even snow tires. There are climbing tires and downhill tires. There are directional tires and omnidirectional tires. So many tires and so little time.

Tire choice is a highly personal and individual thing. Something as simple as looking at tires gets overwhelming pretty quickly. It's enough to send you out of a bike shop screaming, "All I want is a tire!" It's a good idea to think about what you want before you set out. Keep in mind the type of trails that you usually ride or that you want to.

First, you need to know what you're looking at. The tires with the big, nasty looking tread, or "knobbies," are the best for really grabbing and digging in. These are available in two general types of configurations: patterns in which the knobbies are close together for hard conditions like rocks, gravel, and hard-packed dirt, and patterns in which the knobbies are spaced widely apart for soft conditions like powdery dirt, sand and mud.

There are also tires with smaller treads, not nearly as fierce-looking. These are primarily for fast, smooth conditions. If you ride mainly on paved or graveled trails and don't anticipate ever playing it rough, you might want to check these out.

A lot of riders compromise, having a pair of both types of tires on hand to suit their moods and trail conditions; big bad knobbies for the hard core adventures, and low-profile cyclocross or road tires for the spins around town or to the park.

Aside from the size of tire treads, you may also wish to consider the tread patterns. There are tires that have patterns that look almost like arrows or chevrons which all or mostly point in the same direction. These are directional tires. Directional tires are usually put up front, the idea being that they'll go right where you point them and hold your line. Their claim to fame is steering control.

There are tires that have rectangular knobby patterns. Their forte is added traction. The pattern carves a line and holds to it. These are usually used on the back, working in conjunction with a directional front tire.

There are tires that appear to be a combination of arrows and rectangles. These are directional tires that are suitable for both the front and the back, giving you the steering control and the added traction. The arrows should point forward if used on the front and backward on the rear.

There are tires with rounded knobbies or patterns that look like puzzle pieces. These are omni- or multi-directional tires. They give you the traction, leaving the steering control up to the rider.

Next, you need to know what the size means. All mountain bikes have twenty-six inch tires, meaning they are 26 inches in diameter. The width is the number you need to concern yourself with. Widths vary between 1.95 inches and 2.2 inches. The wider the tire, the more ground you cover, which results in more traction.

However, you may sacrifice speed when you opt for the wider tires. If you have racing aspirations, you'd probably want to stay on the narrow side, say 1.95s or 2.0s.

Cathy has a 2.2 inch tire up front with a 2.1 inch tire in the back. The theory behind the different sizes is that the front tire gets a boosted coverage base. This gives your front end more stability and a little added steering control. She has no complaints.

Another popular combo is, obviously, both tires being the same width. This gives a predictable performance, with the front and back ends working together. If you want more traction, use wider tires. If you're more interested in speed, use the narrower ones. Robin, who likes all the traction she can get, has 2.2s mounted on front and back.

You could run a wider tire in back, we suppose, although you run the risk of sacrificing front end traction by doing so. Since the majority of the weight, both the bike's and yours, is centered near the rear, the back tire is all ready getting better traction than the front, making a wider back tire unnecessary.

Lastly, you'll find yourself faced with a choice of rubber compounds. Disregarding one company's proprietary super-soft compound which, although great for traction, doesn't last very long, there are two options: steel bead or Kevlar.

Steel bead tires are the standard; a stiff rubber tread reinforced by steel wire (thus the name) in the rim. These tires tend to lead a long and productive life but are heavier, though not by much — usually an ounce or two, than their more-expensive Kevlar cousins. Traction is dependent largely on size and tread pattern.

Kevlar tires are lighter weight and the rubber is softer. They're often referred to as "folding tires" because you can, literally, fold them up for compact, easy transport in the event that you anticipate changing a tire (as opposed to the tube). Unless you have a history of shredding tires, this feature may not be important.

Kevlar's real specialty is traction; the softer rubber is more pliant which increases the tires' ground contact. The downside is that Kevlar tires are a little more expensive. But, if you can afford it, it's often the tire of choice.

Saddles

If you are looking for higher performance in your riding, you should take a hard look at our next suggested upgrade — a replacement saddle. You will feel a jump in responsive handling and agility the day you switch to an exposed rail or racing saddle.

As we discussed in Chapter 2, the more you ride, the better you can judge what saddle size works best for you. We also noted that wide saddles impair your riding performance. So now we are going to recommend that you give a small performance saddle a try. We like them and think that you will as well.

As you have learned by now, maneuverability is a key to your bike handling skills. Whether you chose a men's or a women's model, a racing saddle gives you more room to move around which increase your reflexes, and in turn, your bike's reflexive response. Not only is the weight difference extremely noticeable, your body is able to completely move in tune with your bike. You'll be able to move in front of or behind the saddle with greater ease, you will find that turns feel less awkward, and you be able to increase your balance and power because your tucked-in body is more in tune with the bike.

Recreational riders will understandably balk at this idea but those of you with racing ambitions or who would simply like to fully master your machine ought to give a racing saddle a whirl.

Suspension Forks

The last essential item, albeit an expensive one, for the shopping list of those intending to spend any length of quality time in the saddle is a suspension fork. The advent of the suspension fork has revolutionized the sport of mountain biking, taking it to new extremes of speed and handling capabilities. But you don't have to be a speed freak to be able to appreciate its benefits.

A suspension fork is a shock absorber for the front wheel. It bears the brunt of the impact from hitting rocks, ruts, logs, roots, or whatever else you happen to run over. The less wear and tear your body is required to take, the longer you're able to ride without getting worn out, but more importantly, the more control you have.

It increases your traction by effectively removing the ricochet effect so that your wheel stays in constant contact with the ground. Suspension is so highly regarded as an idea whose time has definitely come that a lot of mid-range and almost all high-end bikes now come stock with suspension forks.

There are two forms of suspension forks: linkage and telescopic. A linkage fork is comprised of rigid legs, similar to regular forks, attached, or "linked," to the steerer tube via a suspension unit. Telescopic forks are named such because the fork legs have two parts, the inner leg (the "stanchion") and the outer leg (the "slider"). The inner leg slides in and out of the outer leg, like a telescope. This form of suspension fork is, by far, the most popular.

There are three types of telescopic suspension forks currently available. One uses an air and oil combination ("hydraulic"), much like automobile or motorcycle shock absorbers. The oil absorbs the impact while the air pushes against it, creating a rebound. The higher the air pressure, the stiffer the ride.

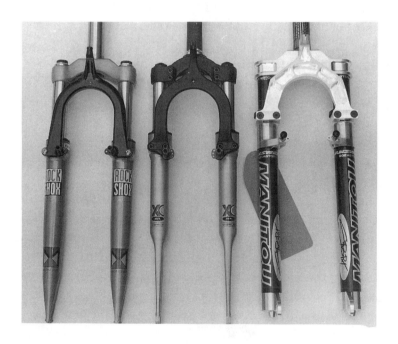

A few examples of telescopic suspension forks.

Why have a stiff riding suspension fork? The stiffness refers to the rate of rebound. A softer setting absorbs the smaller bumps, but bottoms out or rebounds too slowly on the big hits. A stiff setting is for the all-out, heavy duty pounding, basically ignoring the small hits in favor of a faster rebound rate on the big ones.

Heavier riders, like men, for instance, tend to benefit more from stiffer settings as they are the ones adversely affected by the too-soft settings. Soft settings under the pressure of a heavy rider sometimes result in a phenomenon known as biopacing, when the front end of the bike bobs up and down with the pedal strokes. The lighter the rider, the less likely it is that biopacing will be a problem.

The drawback of the air/oil suspension fork is that they require a lot of maintenance to sustain peak performance. You should clean the seals after every ride and periodically check and refill the air, change the oil, and clean the forks inside and out. The positive side is that they can be fine-tuned to fit a rider or style.

The second type of fork uses an elastomer or polymer spring or spring combination. The springs actually look like a cylindrical rubber bumper, like the tip of a doorstop. They are called springs because they absorb and recoil — a bumper only absorbs.

With this type of fork, the absorption and rebound are both controlled by the springs. You adjust the stiffness by either a knob or an allen bolt that twists the bumpers to stiffen their absorption capability. Most elastomer suspension forks allow further fine-tuning by offering a choice of elastomers with different damping rates. The same rule governing stiffness applies here, although the gushiness on a soft setting is not so extreme. The rebound is generally faster than their hydraulic counterparts. These types of forks are typically low maintenance, requiring only periodic cleaning and checking the springs once in a while for undue wear.

The third fork style utilizes both forms of suspension, using an elastomer stack coupled with an oil cartridge. Maintenance is similar to an all-elastomer type fork; the oil cartridge is not serviceable so you replace it as necessary, once a year or so.

A suspension fork is handy in tough terrain.

In all fairness, the manufacturers of each type of fork are making user-friendliness a priority, increasing their fine tuning capabilities and making maintenance as easy as possible.

A word you'll hear often in the same breath as "suspension" is "travel." Travel refers to the compression rate of the suspension system. To completely oversimplify it, the more travel you have, the bigger the hits your fork can smooth out.

When you start looking at suspension forks, right after you notice how cool they look, in an industrial kind of way, you'll discover that their prices can be somewhat...shall we say...high. Your first reaction, after recoiling in horror, will be to laugh heartily and say, "For what?"

If you plan on riding off-road more than two or three times a week, and certainly if the trails you take have a lot of bumps and jolts, a suspension fork is worth the investment. If you doubt their value, test ride a bike with a suspension fork. Better yet, if you know someone with one, try to pry their fingers off their grips long enough to take their bike on your favorite trail. Once you've thrown a leg over a Cadillac ride, it's sort of a let down to get back on your Volkswagen. You'll never look at rigid forks in the same way again.

"The bicycle is really a very simple machine. With a little effort, even a beginning mechanic will find it to be almost intuitively obvious. Principles mastered on one part of the bicycle are readily applicable to other parts."

Georgena Terry
President of Terry Precison Bicycles
For Women, Inc.

Chapter 12

Basic Maintenance

We are not going to ask you to rebuild your bike.

We will, however, provide you with some basic survival tips that will save you money, increase your confidence in your bike, and strengthen your sense of independence. We will teach you how to do something that will not happen very often, something that will, and a basic tune-up.

To those who say they are not mechanically inclined, we say, anyone can perform the tasks that we are about to teach you. First, above all, stay calm. Remember, although they can take a thrashing, bicycle parts are delicate. Never force anything. If you get frustrated, put everything down gently and walk away for a minute or two; longer, if you are at wit's end. Nine times out of ten, when you go back to it after taking a break, you will have no problem.

Let's begin.

Fixing A Flat

Fixing a flat tire is the most common bike repair. At one time or another, all mountain bikers will be called upon to fix one. Flats have a knack for occurring at the most inconvenient times — when the tires are at their muddiest, when the mosquitoes are rampant, or when the rest of your gang is way down the fire trail, waiting. The best thing you can do, for yourself and your riding companions, is run through the drill a few times before getting out on the trail.

Flats are a snap to fix as long as you have the right tools. Remember those tire tools we told you to pack along in Chapter 2? Here's where you learn how to use them. You'll also need to break out the patch kit or inner tube as well as your pump or air cartridge.

Remove the wheel by squeezing the brake shoes against the rim with your hand to reduce the cable tension and unfasten the brake cable. Then flip open the quick release lever, giving the locknut a turn or two to the left. If you're removing the back wheel, make a mental note of which gear the chain is on for the sake of convenience in putting it back. Even easier, lift the wheel and shift the chain to the smallest cog.

Take out one of the tire tools. It should have a flat scoop on one end and a hook on the other. With the tip of the hook or the top of the air valve cap, push against the valve in the air stem to let the majority of the remaining air out of the tire. If you're going to replace the tube, go ahead and let all of the air out.

Using the flat end of a tire tool, gently pry out the lip of the tire from the rim in one spot and, keeping the tire tool in place, fasten the hooked end around the nearest spoke. This gives you an all-important free hand as well as a starting point.

Grab a second tire tool, insert it into the opening you made next to the first one and work your way around the rim, prying the tire out. If it's a little stubborn, let a little more air out of the tube.

Some types of rims are markedly more difficult to deal with than others. If your tire just does not want to come off, lean the wheel against whatever is handy and use two tire tools simultaneously, one in each hand, a couple of inches away from the first tool. This is why tire tools come in threes.

Wedge the two tire levers you are holding into the space between the tire and the rim, about six to eight inches apart, and push down as hard and abruptly as you can. Make sure you have a good grasp on the levers as they have been know to fly under these

Using the tire tools.

circumstances. It may take a couple of tries so don't get discouraged. When the tire pops out, it will expose enough of itself to ease the pressure holding the rest of it in the rim.

When you've got one full side of the tire out of the rim, repeat the procedure on the other side. This side is a piece of cake. The tire, tube, and rim should now be free to go their separate ways.

The easiest way to deal with a flat tire is simply to replace the tube. We strongly recommend carrying both a spare inner tube <u>and</u> a patch kit because lightning can sometimes strike twice, particularly for those riding on thorn-infested trails.

Speaking of which, check the inside of the tire for thorns or other sharp objects. See if you can find out what caused the flat before you replace the tube. Nothing is more frustrating than to fix a flat and have the same thorn puncture the new tube.

After removing the ruined tube, pump a little air into the new one to give it a bit of body which will help keep it in place and out of the way when you put the tire back on. Make sure the air stem is poking all the way through the hole in the rim. It's a good idea to put the cap on it to encourage it to stay put. It's also a good way to not lose the cap. Squeeze the edges of the tire into the rim at the same time. The only hard part will be the last couple of inches on one side. You need to push up as you push in and it'll pop into place.

When you're putting the tire on, regardless of whether you took only one side out or the whole thing, be careful to not pinch or crimp the tube between the tire and rim. Use the tire levers as little as possible, if at all. A tweaked tube will lead to a blowout or pinch flat.

If you're planning on just doing a patch job and you know the general vicinity of the hole, you don't need to take the wheel off the bike. Simply remove about six inches or so of one side of the tire from the rim and gently slip the inner tube out. To find the hole, if you can't see it, squirt a small amount of water around the suspect area. This is why we told you to leave air in the tube. The water will show you exactly where the hole is by making a small bubble or two, or the air may make a high-pitched sound as it escapes through the water, or both.

Once you've found the hole, clean the surrounding area and dry it off. Bear in mind that the area has to be completely dry for the patch to stick. The point here is to remove any dust or dirt that might make the patch fall off.

Open up the patch kit and find the scraper; it will either be a small swatch of sandpaper or something that looks like a grater for the tiniest vegetables in the world. Use this to rough up the surface of the area immediately surrounding the hole. The patch will stick better to an uneven surface, but don't go overboard and rip up what's left of your tube.

Now, using the glue sparingly, apply it to the roughed up surface, allow it a few moments to dry, then slap a patch over the hole. Give it a couple of minutes to completely dry, and voilà. Pop the tire back in the rim and you're nearly done.

Use your pump or cartridge to inflate the tire. The recommended air pressure is imprinted on the side of all tires. Pumping it up to the halfway point between the high and low psi (pounds per square inch) recommendations is a good pressure for most types of riding, generally between 40 and 50 psi. You can even go a little lower for additional traction. Since most people won't have an air gauge handy, squeeze the undamaged tire and try to match it by feel.

Which brings us to our next procedure. In placing the wheel back on the fork, or if you transport your bike by removing the front wheel, you will have this experience: you put the wheel back, lock the quick release, and discover that one of the brake shoes is rubbing against the rim.

Did you break something? Did you accidently change something by releasing the cable pull to take off the wheel? Do you have to fix your brakes? The answer to all of these questions is no. Don't worry, this is relatively easy to fix.

The rubbing (also know as "brake shoe drag") happens because the tension of the quick release inadvertently changed when it was released and now the balance is off-center. A quick release is a spring loaded axle. As you tighten it, the wheel is "pulled" in the direction of the lever because you're compressing the spring on that side which allows it to expand on the other side.

Fiddling with the quick release.

To move the wheel away from the brake shoe, you need to loosen the skewer on the same side as that of the touching brake shoe. At the same time, you need to tighten the opposite end, "pulling" the wheel in that direction. It takes some back-and-forth fiddling to get it just right. As you work with it, periodically lift the front end of the bike by the fork to allow the wheel free movement.

Once you have the wheel centered again, with both brake shoes off the rim, snap the lever back to its upright locked position. If there's a lot of resistance, you need to loosen the locknut by a half-turn or so. Trying to force the quick release to lock can damage or even break the axle.

Never lock either of your quick releases with the lever pointing down or forward. They'll stand a good chance of getting caught on something and opening up at inopportune moments. The next bump you hit may send your wheel on ahead without you. Fiddle with it as much as necessary to make it lock securely, pointing up.

Tune-ups

And now we come to the pièce de résistance: the basic tune-up. The term "tune-up" sounds a lot more technical and intimidating than it is. A bicycle tune-up is a simple, three-part process; cleaning, lubrication, and tightening. That's all there is to it. We'll take it one step at a time.

Step One: cleaning. If you get a tune-up done at a bike shop, they'll only do the most essential cleaning so it's up to you to give you bike the attention it deserves. Have at your disposal three rags, some water, and a chain lube. We also like to have an old toothbrush handy for getting at the grime in between the gears and in the derailleurs, but we have been called fanatics. Designate a rag as the damp rag, another as the dry rag, and the last as the oil rag.

If you don't have a bike stand (a nice thing to add to your wish list), turn your bike upside down, letting it rest on the handlebars and seat. Dampen the so-designated rag with water and wipe off everything that's not greasy. That includes the frame, the fork legs, the cables, the brake assembly; everything but the chainrings, chain, and the freewheel.

If your bike's a little muddy, give the mud a chance to dry. Then you can brush it off in nice, orderly clumps. If it's a muddy mess, hose it down, using a gentle stream setting, keeping the spray away from the headset, (the area where the fork and the handlebar stem meet the frame in the front), the bottom bracket (which is where the pedal arms go into the frame at the bottom), and the rear hub (which holds all the gears together in the center of the rear wheel.) These areas are sensitive to water because they house bearings packed in grease. These are the bearings that keep the attached parts turning smoothly.

Those not living in particularly arid regions should avoid using excessive water. Unless you've splurged on an aluminum frame with an all-aluminum drivetrain complete with sealed bearings and alloy bolts, rust can do a number on your bike. And keep the water pressure to a minimum, the force could drive dirt into unsealed bearing units which will result in the need for an overhaul or replacement.

After you've wiped or hosed everything off, go over everything again with the dry rag. Again, special attention should be paid to the headset and bottom bracket. Because of their internal grease, the headset and bottom bracket are natural collecting points for dust and dirt particles. Care should be taken to keep their outer surfaces as clean as possible.

It's also a good idea to occasionally clean your rims and brake pads. If you have silver rims, you'll notice that there are black streaks running along the surface. These are from the brake pads. A steel wool pad or fine sand paper, with a little elbow grease, takes the residue right off. If your brakes have been on the noisy side, you need to clean them. To clean your brake pads, release the cable and, with steel wool or sand paper, give each pad a light rubdown.

Now that they are clean, you can easily check the pads for wear by noting the depth of the ridges. They start off being a little over 1/8 of an inch deep; as the pads get worn down, the ridges get more shallow. They should be replaced when the wear is significant, certainly before it reaches the halfway point. If they wear out on the trail, you may damage your expensive metal rims.

Now the chain and gears must look really dirty, compared to the frame and all the other non-greasy parts. With your oil rag, wipe off the chainrings and rear cluster gears as much as possible. This part takes a little patience because you can really gouge your fingers by going too fast. The gears are sharper than they look. As we mentioned before, we sometimes use a toothbrush to get to those hard-to-reach areas.

Cleaning the chain.

Now that chain must look really bad. Hold the chain firmly but loosely in the rag and turn one of the pedals forward. Keep turning it until you've wiped off all the gook and you can actually see all of the metal links. This is the way the pros clean chains. You can also use one of the chain cleaning devices that are now available, but this way is the easiest.

While you're cleaning the chain, you'll probably notice that there are two pulleys, about the size of fifty cent pieces, in the rear derailleur that guide the chain — and they're simply filthy. Take the oil rag and pinch each pulley, still turning that pedal, to get rid of the grime build up.

Now you're ready to for Step Two: lubrication. Bike shops are the place to find bike lubricants. They come in one of two formulas: all-purpose and dry. All-purpose lube is pretty self-explanatory; it's a Teflon-based oil, suitable for all types of riding conditions. Dry lube, besides lubricating also coats with a paraffin-like layer to repel foreign particles and thus is great for dry and dusty conditions. Lubrication is another subjective area. Some people swear by one kind, some by the other, and some people use both. We like both.

Lubricants also come in two applications: drip bottles or sprays. Everyone we've talked to agrees that using the bottles nullifies the chance of accidentally spraying the back tire rim, also known as the braking surface.

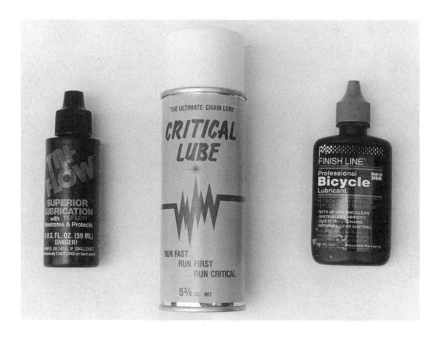

Examples of lubricants.

There are three areas requiring lubrication: the chain, the pivot points, and the cables. First the chain. Apply a drop or two of lubricant on each link from chainring to gear. You don't need to drown it, a little really does go a long way. Then turn the pedal and do the next section. Keep repeating this until the whole chain is oiled. Then, once again holding the chain loosely with the rag, turn the pedal for a couple of minutes to wipe away the excess lubricant so things don't get gunked up too quickly.

Lubing the chain.

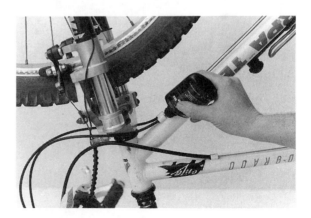

Lubing the cables.

Even if you don't clean your bike very often, you should clean and lube your chain every few rides. This will extend the life of your chain and ensure smooth shifting performance.

The next areas needing a little lube and affection are the pivot points. These are the hinges in the derailleurs that make the derailleur respond swiftly to your shifting commands. There are four hinges on each derailleur, two on the outside, and two in the back. They're not greedy, all they want is a drop or two to make them happy. Again, wipe away any excess lube to discourage dirt from using the pivot points as a gathering place.

The last step in the lubrication process is to apply a drop to the cables at the point where the exposed metal part disappears into the plastic housings. For those whose rear brake and gear shift cables are routed under the bottom bracket, a drop or two on the cable and cable guide will keep the elements from shortening your cables' life span. Again, remove any excess lubricant.

Now you know what's meant by "a well-oiled machine." People are talking about your bike.

Which brings us, finally, to Step Three: tightening. Go over the bike from one end to the other and check that every allen bolt is tight. Your bike is constantly getting jostled and jarred which can shake things loose. If you can fit an allen wrench in it, tighten it. The exception (aren't there always exceptions?) is the adjustment bolt on the top of your brake lever housing. This is to adjust the span of the lever; it brings the lever closer to the handlebar.

When you're hunting for places to use your allen wrench, you'll probably notice two little screws sticking out of your derailleurs. Don't touch these. They are adjusting screws that manipulate the angle of the derailleurs. Once you alter them, it may take you days of fine tuning and test riding to get them set right again. Just a little friendly advice — it's probably best to leave that work to the folks at the bike shop.

So, there you have it. You've just done a tune-up. And the great thing is, you now have an intimate working knowledge of your mountain bike. Besides, sometimes it's fun to get your hands dirty.

Post Script

The information contained in this book is based on experience, opinion, and advice. Neither of us are professional riders nor are we trained in any health or medical capacity.

This book is not meant to be construed as the last word in mountain biking. If we've served our purpose well, it's only the beginning.

Happy Trails,

Robin & Cathy

Glossary of Bike Terms

Aftermarket — Sold individually, as in "an aftermarket handlebar"

Armor — protective gear typically worn by downhill racers which includes full-face helmets and hip, knee, shoulder, and elbow pads.

Beartrap pedal — the pedals on many mountain bikes which are sized to provide more contact with the foot and have ridges to keep your shoe from sliding off.

Bottom bracket — the workhorse section of the crank assembly consisting of a spindle, bearings, several bearing cups and adjustment rings. Expensive bikes have sealed bearing cups or cartridges to keep water and dirt out.

Braze-on — brackets and attachments built into a bike for attaching water bottle cages, derailleurs, and brakes.

Brazing — the process, similar to welding, that is used to join bike frame tubes together. Special torches and brass rods are used to keep from deforming the fragile tubing.

Bunny hop — a maneuver to jump over obstacles.

Cantilever brake — most mountain bikes have this type as opposed to the weaker side-pull brake used on road bikes.

Cannibalize — to exchange parts from one bike to another.

Chainring — part of the crank unit. Most mountain bikes have three with the smallest having 20 to 28 teeth, the middle ring from 32 to 40 teeth, and the outer ring 42 to 60 teeth.

City bike — hybrid; also refers to a "beat around town" type of bike that one can afford (emotionally, financially, or both) to have stolen or damaged.

Chromoly — a steel alloy, chromium molybdenum, that is favored by bicycle builders.

Clean — a term used to successfully ride a difficult trail, such as to "clean" a section in an observed trials competition.

Component — other than the frame, anything on a bike such as brakes, wheels, and derailleurs.

Crankset — two crank arms and a bottom bracket form the crank. Attach some pedals and you're ready to roll.

Criterium — a mountain bike race on a short closed course.

Dab — when the foot or hand touches the ground in trials riding. The rider is assessed one point for each dab.

Drivetrain — front and rear derailleurs, shifters, crank arms, bottom bracket, chainrings, rear wheel hub and gears, chain, and pedals.

Dropout — the "notched" part of the bike frame which holds the wheel in place.

Doubletrack,
Duotrack — trail wide enough to accommodate two riders, side by side.

Endo — the act of flying over one's handlebars, end over end.

Fireroad — wide multi-use trail utilized by rangers and emergency vehicles.

Frameset — the frame and the fork. If you are into $2,000 bikes, normally you will buy a frameset from a custom builder and purchase components to complete the bike.

Freewheel — the set of seven or eight chain sprockets mounted on the rear wheel.

Front derailleur — the mechanism that moves the chain from one chain ring to another on the crank. Located near the bottom of the seat tube.

Gauge — the thickness or thinness of the bike frame tubing or of a wheel spoke. The larger the number, the thinner the gauge, for example, a 12-gauge spoke is thicker than a 15-gauge one.

Geometry — the seat tube and steering tube angles and dimensions that affect the maneuverability of a bike.

Gnarly — trails and or riding conditions that are very challenging.

Granny gears — the larger sized gears on the freewheel cluster that allow the rider to spin easily while climbing.

Gruppo — a group of components made by one manufacturer, such as a Shimano gruppo. (Pronounced "group-o")

Hammer — to ride fast and hard.

High-end — expensive, high performance bikes and components.

Hybrid — bicycle with a frame style similar to a road bike with mountain bike style handlebar, shifters, gearing, and wheels.

Indexed shifting — a shifting system found on many mountain bikes which produces a click as the shift lever is moved from one position to the next. An accurate, easy way to shift.

Knobby — off-road tire with treads designed to provide traction in dirt and sand.

Low-end — lesser quality (i.e., heavy and less durable than average) bikes and components.

Mid-range — Bikes and components of average or median price and performance level.

Pilot — rider.

Portage — to carry one's bike.

Quads — quadriceps; outer muscle of the thigh.

Quick release — a lever and cam arrangement that allows easy removal of wheels and easy adjustment of the seat height.

Rear derailleur — moves the chain from one gear to the other on the freewheel cluster on the rear wheel.

Road bike — bicycle with tall front triangle, large diameter wheels, skinny tires, and drop-style curving handlebars.

Roadie — one who rides exclusively on pavement.

Saddle — seat.

Scoot, mount, steed, ride (noun) — bike.

Seat post — the tube to which the seat is connected.

Seat tube — the tube that holds the seat post and continues down to the bottom bracket.

Schrader valve — the tire valve, used for autos and recreational bicycles, that is used for mountain bikes as well. Road bikes and more and more mountain bike tires use a smaller Presta tube valve.

Shoes — tires, except as in "brake shoes."

Shred — to ride a difficult section aggressively, to "shred the trail."

Singletrack — highly coveted narrow trail accommodating riders, single file.

Sneaker — a mountain bike tire, also called a knobby.

Spin — pedal easily.

Technical riding — terrain such as narrow trails, rocky sections, loose sand or mud that requires skill in bike handling.

Trials — also called Observed Trials. An event where riders maneuver through obstacle courses. Points are assessed for dabs and falls with the lowest score winning.

Toe clips — units shaped out of plastic or metal with straps to keep the foot on the pedals.

Trick — a mountain bike term of praise used to describe unique or unusual components or design, such as "the geometry and paint job of her new bike is trick."

Upgrade — to add or replace components (or frame) with those of higher quality.

Washboard — a rippled road condition that is prevalent on hilly dirt roads.

Water bar — a diagonal ditch cut about 30 degrees to the road to divert water and to slow erosion. The deep ones are called tank traps.

Resources

Here are those addresses we promised you. These organizations are here to help. If you'd like information on what you can do to save a trail or two, trail building, general information on the trails that are open and available to you and your off-road compadres, or for referrals to local club affiliates or chapters, simply write or call:

International Mountain Bike Association (IMBA)
P.O. Box 412043
Los Angeles, California 90041
(818) 792-8830

Bureau of Land Management (BLM)
Main Interior Building
MS 7644
1849 C Street N.W.
Washington, D.C. 20240
(202) 208-4662

For information on joining WOMBATS, write:

WOMBATS
Box 757
Fairfax, CA 94978

or call the Batline: (415) 459-0980 West Coast
                    (203) 268-2671 East Coast

For information on converted railroad corridors in your backyard or across the country, write:

Rails-To-Trails Conservancy
1400 Sixteenth Street N.W.
Suite 300
Washington, D.C. 20036

For your racing needs including information, licenses, or memberships, write or call:

National Off-Road Bicycle Association (NORBA)
One Olympic Plaza
Colorado Springs, Colorado 80909
(719) 578-4717

For information on touring or vacation planning, write or call the following (check mountain biking magazines for more):

Alaska Women of the Wilderness
Box 773556
Eagle River, AK 99577
(907) 688-2226

Backroads
1516 5th Street, Ste. W
Berkeley, CA 94710-1740
(800) 533-2573

Odyssey Adventures
305 Commercial Street, Ste. 505
Portland, ME 04101
(800) 544-3216

Recreational Equipment, Inc. (REI)
P.O. Box 1938
Sumner, WA 98390-0800
(800) 622-2236

Roads Less Traveled
P.O. Box 8187
Longmont, CO 80501
(303) 678-8750

Timberline Bicycle Tours
7975 E. Harvard, #J
Denver, CO 80231
(303) 759-3804

Vermont Bicycle Touring
Box 711
Bristol, VT 05443
(802) 453-4811

WOMANTREK
Worldwide Travel Adventures for Women
P.O. Box 20643
Seattle, WA 98102
(206) 325-4772

Index